SUFI ESSAYS

Works by the same author in European languages

Three Muslim Sages

An Introduction to Islamic Cosmological Doctrines

Ideals and Realities of Islam

Islamic Studies

Science and Civilization in Islam

The Encounter of Man and Nature: The Spiritual Crisis of Modern Man

in collaboration with H. Corbin, *Histoire de la Philosophie Islamique*

translation and edition with notes of ‘Allâmah Sayyid Muḥammad Ḥusayn Ṭabâṭabâ’î, *Shi’ite Islam*, in press

SUFI ESSAYS

by

Seyyed Hossein Nasr

State University of New York Press
Albany

Published by State University of New York Press
99 Washington Avenue, Albany, New York 12210

First published 1972 by George Allen & Unwin Ltd

Library of Congress Cataloging in Publication Data
Nasr, Seyyed Hossein
Sufi essays
1. Sufism—Addresses, essays, lectures. I. Title

BP189.N38 1973 297'.4 72-11586

ISBN 0-87395-233-2

Printed in Great Britain

Iḥsân (Sufism):

الاحسان ان تعبد الله كانك تراه فان لم تكن تراه فانه يراك

Iḥsân is to adore Allah as though thou didst see Him, and if thou dost not see Him he nonetheless seeth thee.

Prophetic tradition (*ḥadîth*)

CONTENTS

In the Name of Allah, Most Merciful and Compassionate

INTRODUCTION

For numerous reasons, some positive and many negative, there is much interest in Sufism today in the West and also a resurgence of interest in it among the modern educated classes in the Islamic world itself. The falling apart of the more or less homogeneous 'value system' of the modern world; a sense of insecurity concerning the future; an incomprehension of the messages of the religions prevalent in the West and especially of Christianity, whose inner teachings have become increasingly inaccessible; the desire for a vision of the spiritual world within an environment that is becoming more and more lacking in quality, and many other factors have all contributed to a quest for the spiritual teachings of the Oriental religions. This search in the West began a generation ago with the more general interest in Hinduism and Buddhism; but because so much of what was written and even put into practice during this period was either counterfeit or at best superficial, interest in these traditions—more particularly in the study of the Vedanta and Zen—soon developed into a fad which, for a generation seeking ever new and changing experiences without penetrating deeply into any of them, became rapidly boring and tiresome.

For many the object of attraction has now become Sufism, which alas seems thus bound in turn to be distorted and mutilated to suit the mentality of those who are either innocent, but ignorant of the real nature of a spiritual way, or are purposefully seeking to reduce the sublimest truths to their own petty natures. But along with this more advertised interest in Sufism can be discerned a more profound and genuine attraction by both those who wish to profit from its insights for their spiritual benefit, whatever the religion or spiritual way they are following, and those who are seeking a genuine spiritual path to follow and are willing to make the necessary sacrifices to become qualified to follow such a path.

Among official scholars of Islam in the West can be seen a growing realization of the central role played by Sufism in Islam and Islamic history. Many are now willing to accept the Islamic origin of Sufism and the unbreakable link connecting Sufism to Islam, rather than following the older practice of explaining Sufism away as some kind of alien influence within Islam. One can hardly write of Islamic spirituality today without some consideration of Sufism, although certain orientalists persist in trying to do so.

Whether then it be genuine spiritual interest, or the pseudo-spirituality so prevalent in the West today, or scholarly activity in the field of Islamic studies, one can see the growing significance of Sufism and interest in its study in the West. Authentic presentations of Sufism in modern Western media are rare, while those who seek its teachings are many. The presence of this situation is itself a cogent argument for making all possible efforts to prevent the distortion of the teachings of Sufism and for presenting all its different facets in an authentic form. Sufi wisdom covers nearly every aspect of the spiritual life and represents one of the most complete and well-preserved metaphysical and esoteric traditions that has survived in the modern world.

In the thirteenth[1]/nineteenth century the Islamic world was affected by the impact of the West coupled with the rise of indigenous puritanical movements of a rationalist and anti-mystical kind. There came into being an opposition to Sufism, which was blamed for nearly everything that some of the modernists felt was wrong with the Islamic world at that time. The problem of the domination of the Muslim world by European powers was often blamed on Sufism, and there appeared a generation of Westernized Muslims, still to be found in many Muslim countries today, who considered the very study of Sufism to be a colonialist conspiracy. Aided by the activity of certain orientalists, this movement sought to revive Islam by rejecting all the spiritual and metaphysical aspects of its teachings, reducing it to the narrowest possible interpretation of the Divine Law or *Sharî'ah*. As a result the *Sharî'ah* itself became helpless against the 'intellectual' onslaught of the West.

The positive role played by Sufism in Islamic history—in domains ranging from government to art—came to be overlooked and brushed aside. Strangely enough Western accounts of the modern period of Islamic history also remain singularly silent on all the important reform movements within Sufism itself during the thirteenth/nineteenth century, although the effects of these are certainly not less than those of the Western-orientated modernist movements so emphasized in contemporary European studies. With the exception of the Sanûsiyyah Order, practically nothing has been said of the major

[1] This date refers to the Islamic *hijrah* (A.H.) calendar.

importance of such Sufi revivals as those of the Darqâwiyyah and Tîjâniyyah in North Africa, the Yashrûṭiyyah in East Africa and the Arab Near East, the Ni'matullâhiyyah in Persia and Southern India and the Chishtiyyah and Qâdiriyyah Orders in the Indo-Pakistani sub-continent. Silence in this matter helped belittle Sufism in the eyes of the modern Muslim educated classes, so often dependent on Western sources for the study of their own history.

Thus it is that until around the end of the Second World War one nearly always found only two kinds of students in universities in the more modernized Muslim countries: those who were completely secularized and Westernized and more or less rejected Islam, at least as a complete code and way of life; and those who were very pious and devout Muslims but who limited Islam to the most outward interpretation of the *Sharî'ah* and rejected all that pertains to Sufism and the whole intellectual and spiritual dimension of Islam. Although these two groups were opposed to each other in nearly every way, they were united in their opposition to Sufism.

Today, while much of this attitude persists in these two groups, a marked new interest in Sufism and the whole intellectual dimension of Islam is to be discerned among students and other members of the educated classes in many Muslim countries. The disintegration of Western cultural values and disenchantment with the experiences of modernism, the observation of the catastrophes brought about by modern civilization and anticipation of more to come, and the realization that the challenges and threats posed for Islam by the West in the intellectual domain cannot be answered save through the guidelines provided by the teachings of Sufism have all contributed to this change in attitude. In comparison with the older generation there is a notable rise in the number of youths attracted to Sufi orders and to a study of Sufism in countries as diverse as Egypt, Syria and Persia. In the Indo-Pakistani sub-continent interest continues to be strong, never having diminished in a noticeable manner as was the case in the Arab world and Turkey. In Turkey interest in Sufi writings among university students has increased immensely since the years following the Turkish revolution.

Strangely enough genuine expositions of Sufism adapted for modern educated people in the Islamic world are also rare. In the attitude towards Sufism, as towards Islam itself, one can discern today three classes of people: the traditional majority, whose intellectual elite comprises on different levels the *'ulamâ'* and the Sufi masters and advanced adepts, who can comprehend the traditional expositions of Islamic doctrine on either the Shari'ite or Sufi level; the Westernized minority, who have for the most part shown little interest in Sufism until now; and finally the new modern educated minority which is becoming once again keenly interested in the spiritual and intellectual heritage of Islam.

A vast number of books containing Sufi texts appear annually, for the most part in Arabic and Persian, but also in Turkish, Urdu, Bengali and other Muslim languages. But except for the Sufi poetry of such men as Ibn al-Fâriḍ, Jalâl al-Dîn Rûmî and Ḥâfiẓ, which reach and are appreciated by all of the people, works of Sufism that are of a doctrinal nature and contain the intellectual instructions of Sufism are addressed only to the qualified few and cannot be fully understood except by the intellectual elite (*khawâṣṣ*) of the traditional classes. One wonders how many modern educated Arabs, Turks and Persians understand the text of the *Fuṣûṣ al-ḥikam* of Ibn 'Arabî, the *Manâqib al-'ârifîn* of al-Aflâkî or the *Sharḥ-i gulshan-i râz* of Lâhîjî, which have been published in Egypt, Turkey and Persia respectively during the past few years. When all of the 'isms' that pour in from the West like a flood, such as evolutionism, Marxism, socialism etc., strike the soil of the Islamic world, how many of the Muslim educated classes can draw from the immensely rich heritage of Islamic metaphysics, philosophy and Sufism to protect themselves and prevent themselves from being drowned? A few have contact with the still living spiritual masters, from whom they draw their sustenance. The majority remain bewildered and have no access to anything but a few books written by their contemporary and compatriot scholars, who usually do no more than emulate Western orientalists. Genuine contemporary expositions and profound interpretations of Sufism in Muslim languages could probably be counted on the fingers of two hands, and thus this new interest in Sufism among the educated classes finds very few works with which to satisfy itself.

Moreover, many Muslims now study in the West and strangely enough feel more at home in English or French than in their mother tongue when it comes to discussing intellectual matters. Even in some Muslim countries, such as Malaysia, Pakistan, Nigeria and Muslim North Africa, English and French are still more important instruments of intellectual discourse than Malay, Urdu and Bengali, the Nigerian languages or Arabic. In these cases, it is the expositions of Sufism in European languages that serve as the most immediate source to satiate the ever-increasing thirst for knowledge in this field.

The trends in the two worlds, Muslim and Western, thus seem to meet as far as the need for authentic studies of Sufism is concerned. For very different reasons both the Muslim intelligentsia and a good number of the most intelligent among Western youth, as well as people of other age groups, are becoming ever more interested in Sufism, some as a fad, others superficially, and still others for the deepest reasons of a soul struggling to save itself from the abyss of meaninglessness. Yet, the studies that succeed in unveiling in an authentic manner those verities of Sufism that can be divulged are rare indeed, so that people with the purest of intentions are often led, through the reading of works of falsification, towards the infernal depths of the 'lower worlds', rather than towards the celestial heights they are seeking.

Today in the West one can distinguish three types of writing on Sufism. The scholarly works of orientalists range from the most damaging and prejudiced criticisms of some authors to the sympathetic and often penetrating studies of such men as L. Massignon, H. Corbin, E. Dermenghem, L. Gardet, C. Rice, F. Meier and P. Filipanni-Ronconi, which border in some cases on actual participation in the world of Sufism and which include excellent translations by men like B. de Sacy, R. A. Nicholson and A. J. Arberry. There are also works claiming to be associated with different current Sufi movements in the West, works which often contain many genuine teachings of the founder of the movement but which have become intermingled with all kinds of extraneous matters, making the sifting of the wheat from the chaff difficult, especially for the beginner. Such works have lately gained an occultist tinge and become completely divorced from Islam in certain circles that have sprung up in Western Europe, especially in England. Finally, there are the truly authentic expositions of Sufism emanating from genuine teachings, such as those of R. Guénon, M. Lings, J. L. Michon, L. Schaya, and especially F. Schuon and T. Burckhardt; these are few in number but of the greatest importance for an authentic understanding of Sufism. A few genuine works of contemporary Sufi masters of the Muslim world have also appeared in English or French, but usually in a form that leaves much to be desired. The person who already knows the principles of Sufism can make use of the documentation, explanation and translations of the works in the first group, and even some of the sayings, tales and accounts of certain of the books in the second group. But to do so he must have keen insight and an effective knowledge of the metaphysical doctrines which only the third category of works or direct contact with the authentic sources of Sufism can provide.

It is therefore essential to increase the number of works of an authentic nature on Sufism. And this not merely with a quantitative goal in mind, but also with the aim of providing a greater variety of keys for the different types of seekers and of making accessible in a contemporary medium at least an inkling of the vast field covered by the traditional teachings of Sufism. This task must be accomplished with consideration for both the Western audience, who would naturally benefit most from an exposition in a European language, and also the Western-educated Muslim for whom a Western language is in many cases the channel for the reception of most of his ideas. It is with both these audiences in mind that these humble essays have been brought together in book form, in the hopes of making a small contribution to the corpus of expositions of Sufism from a Sufi point of view that have now begun to appear in European languages.

In the Holy Quran God refers to Himself as the Outward (*al-ẓâhir*) and the Inward (*al-bâṭin*). Inasmuch as this world and all that is in it are reflections and theophanies of the Names and Qualities of God, all the realities of this world also possess an outward and an inward aspect. The outward face of things is not sheer illusion; it has a reality on its own level. But it implies a movement in the direction of separation and withdrawal from the Principle that resides at the Centre and may be identified with the Inward. To live in the outward is to possess already the blessing of existence, to be more than nothing. But to remain satisfied solely with the outward is to betray the very nature of man, whose profoundest reason for existence is precisely to journey from the outward to the inward, from the periphery of the circle of existence to the Transcendent Centre and in so doing to return creation to its origin.

Sufism provides the means for the accomplishment of this supreme end. God has made the journey from the outward to the inward possible through revelation, which in itself comprises both the outward and inward dimensions. In Islam this inward or esoteric dimension of the revelation corresponds for the most part to Sufism, although, in the context of Shi'ism, Islamic esotericism has also manifested itself in other forms. Moreover, from the Islamic point of view something corresponding to Sufism exists in every integral revelation or tradition in conformity with the nature of things. That is why in Islamic languages one often refers to the 'Sufism' of this or that religion, for from the Islamic point of view, *taṣawwuf*, like *al-dîn* or *al-islâm* in their universal sense, is both perennial and universal. But this does not imply in any way that it is possible to practise Sufism outside the framework of Islam—in whatever context we use these terms. If we mean by *al-islâm* religion in its universal sense, then the type of esotericism (or *taṣawwuf*, to use the terminology of the Sufis themselves) that is practised must belong to the particular religion or *'islâm'* from which it has sprung. And if we mean by *al-islâm* the religion revealed through the Holy Quran, then likewise the *taṣawwuf* which may be legitimately practised must be the one that has its roots in the Quranic revelation and which we call 'Sufism' in the general acceptation of this term. In any case a valid esoteric way is inseparable from the objective framework of the revelation to which it belongs. One cannot practise Buddhist esotericism in the context of the Islamic *Sharî'ah* or vice versa. Furthermore, one cannot claim under any circumstances to stand above the exoteric teachings of religion and to practice an esotericism without them and in the void, any more than one can plant a tree in the middle of the air. One can journey toward God only as a part of the sacred humanity (*ummah*), or 'mystical body' to use the term of Christian theology, which God has formed and sanctified through a revelation that has reached mankind through His Will. The Islamic teaching that all men who enter Paradise do so as part of the 'people' (*ummah*) of a particular prophet refers to the same truth.

To follow Sufism is to die gradually to oneself and to become one-Self, to be born anew and to become aware of what one has always been from eternity (*azal*) without one's having realized it until the necessary transformation has come about. It means to glide out of one's own mould like a snake peeling off its skin. Such a transformation implies a profound transmutation of the very substance of the soul through the miraculous effect of the Divine Presence (*ḥuḍûr*) that is implanted in the heart through initiation by the spiritual master and which is efficacious thanks to the grace (*barakah*) that flows from the origin of the revelation itself. In order that this transformation may take place there must be a traditional link with the origin or a spiritual chain (*silsilah*), a discipline or method to train the soul, a master who can apply the method and who can guide (*irshâd*) the disciple through the stations of the journey and finally a knowledge of a doctrinal order about the nature of things which will give direction to the adept during his spiritual journey (*sayr wa sulûk*). And of course as a pre-requisite there must be a formal initiation (*bay'ah*) which attaches the disciple to the master and his spiritual chain as well as to the higher orders of being. These are the fundamental aspects of Sufism.

To expound the teachings of Sufism fully one must give at least an outline of Sufi doctrine, which includes a metaphysics about the principle and nature of things, a cosmology concerning the structure of the Universe and its multiple states of being, a traditional psychology about the structure of the human soul to which is attached a psychotherapy of the profoundest order compared to which modern psychotherapy is but a caricature, and finally an eschatology concerning the final end of man and of the Universe and man's posthumous becoming. The elucidation of the teachings of Sufism would include, moreover, a discussion of the spiritual methods, their manner of administration and the way in which they take root in the very substance of the soul of the disciple. It would also involve a discussion of the relation between master and disciple and of the spiritual virtues, which are engendered in the soul of the disciple through the alchemy performed upon his soul by the master.

Besides Sufi poetry, which usually contains images of different attitudes and spiritual states (*aḥwâl*) of the soul in quest of the Divine, nearly all Sufi treatises concern one or more of the points outlined above. Some are more clearly doctrinal, others more practical; yet others are descriptive and attempt to paint an image to be emulated rather than give direct instructions. The vast literature of Sufism in all the Islamic languages, of which the Arabic and Persian occupy the central position of prominence but of which also many other Muslim languages such as Turkish, Urdu, Bengali and Sindhi provide important elements, is like an ocean full of waves which move in different directions and are of different forms but always return to that primeval ground from which they have originated. This monumental literature is forever fresh and timely because it is inspired. The masters of Sufism have all said essentially the same thing throughout the ages, yet their words are different. They are new creations suited for the different peoples addressed and based upon a fresh vision of spiritual reality by their creators. They are like the new day, which is the same as the day before yet fresh and inspiring. Authentic Sufi writings are at once the 'horizontal' continuation of a transmitted knowledge that has passed from one generation to another going back to the origin of Islam and a 'vertical', fresh vision of the Truth, which stands at the same time at the origin and beginning of the revelation and at the Centre of our being here and now.

Because it is like the breath that animates the body, Sufism has infused its spirit into the whole structure of Islam in both its social and intellectual manifestations. The orders of the Sufis, being well-organized bodies within the larger matrix of Islamic society, have exerted influences of an enduring and profound nature upon the whole structure of society, albeit their primary function has been to safeguard the spiritual disciplines and make possible their propagation from one generation to another. Moreover, secondary initiatic organizations have been affiliated with Sufism throughout Islamic history, ranging from the knightly orders which used to guard the frontiers of Islam and which were known in their different forms as the orders of the *ghâzîs* or the *jawânmards*, which latter are associated with the *zûrkhânah* in Persia, to guilds and different artisanal groups associated with the *futuwwât* and the personality of 'Ali ibn Abî Ṭâlib. No study in depth of Islamic society is possible without taking into consideration the action of these 'societies within society', especially during periods when the outer social structure became weakened as for example after the Mongol invasion in the eastern lands of Islam. Nor are many of the problems of Islamic history, such as the spread of Islam into Asia or the transformation of Persia from a predominantly Sunni to a Shi'ite country, understandable without recourse to the basic role played by Sufism.

In the field of education also the role of Sufism has been profound, for the central task of Sufism is the education of the whole of the human person until it reaches the full realization and perfection of all of its possibilities. The direct participation of many Sufis such as Khwâjah Niẓâm al-Mulk, the Seljuq vizier, in the establishment of universities or *madrasahs* as well as the role of the Sufi centres (*zâwiyah* in Arabic, *khâniqâh* in Persian) in the administration of education makes the influence of Sufism inseparable from the development of education in Islam. Again, during certain periods such as the post-Mongol period when the formal educational system was destroyed in certain regions, the Sufi centres remained the sole depository of even formal and academic knowledge and the basis from which the traditional schools sprang up once again.

In the field of the arts and sciences the influence of Sufism has been enormous. The author has already sought to show in another work how closely the tradition of Sufism is related to the cultivation of the sciences, even those of nature, in Islam.[2] In nearly every form of the arts, ranging from poetry to architecture, the affinity with Sufism is even more marked. The Sufis live even in this life in what one might call the front courtyard of Paradise, and hence breathe in a climate of spiritual splendour whose beauty is reflected in all that they say or do or make. Islam itself is deeply attached to the aspect of the Divinity as beauty, and this feature is particularly accentuated in Sufism, which quite naturally is derived from and contains what is essential in Islam. It is not accidental that the works written by Sufis, whether they be poetry or prose, are of great literary quality and beauty.

[2] See S. H. Nasr, *Science and Civilization in Islam*, Cambridge (Mass.), 1968 and New York, 1970.

In the field of Islamic literature what is most universal belongs to the domain of Sufism. It was the spirit of Sufism that raised Arabic and Persian literature from local lyric and at most epic verse to a didactic and mystical literature of the most universal dimensions, enriching Arabic most of all in the prose form and Persian in the poetic. Moreover, many of the more local Islamic languages reached their apogee in the hands of Sufi writers: the very genius of Sindhi, for example, seems to have been exhausted by a single Sufi poet, Shâh 'Abd al-Laṭîf. Like Italian and German, which in a sense owe their birth to the mystics Dante and Eckhart, many of the Muslim languages owe their very development and subsistance as Muslim languages to the genius of Sufi poets.

Nearly the same situation can be observed in the fields of music, architecture, calligraphy, miniature etc. Many of the outstanding Muslim architects have been attached to Sufism through the guilds of masons and builders. Similarly many of the masters of calligraphy and miniature have been affiliated with Sufism, often even more directly, in the sense that they have belonged in many cases directly to a Sufi order rather than to a particular guild which is in turn connected with an order. As for music, it is legitimate in Islam only in the form of the spiritual concerts (*samâ'*) practiced in Sufism, so that the tradition of classical music, Arabic and Persian as well as Turkish, has been cultivated over the centuries mostly by those attached to Sufism and in Sufi gatherings. Furthermore, since the days of Amîr Khusraw many of the most outstanding masters of North Indian music have been Muslims, and this is still the case even today. Certain developments in Indian music are connected directly to the theory and practise of Sufism and many of the Muslim masters of Indian music have been attached in one way or another to the Sufi orders of the subcontinent. The Sufis are the people of sapiential knowledge and vision or *dhawq*; moreover, not by any means accidentally in Arabic and Persian this same *dhawq* means also good taste and discernment in art. The Sufis have been the cultivators of the arts, not because this is a goal of the Sufi path but because to follow Sufism is to become ever more aware of the Divine Beauty which manifests itself everywhere and in the light of which the Sufi makes things of beauty in conformity with the beauty of his own nature and also according to the traditional artistic norms, which reflect the Beauty of the Supreme Artisan.

In order to expound all aspects of Sufism in contemporary language and also in an authentic manner, a task much called for in both East and West, it would be necessary to treat not only of all the different facets of Sufism itself as outlined above, but also of all the major manifestations of Sufism in Islamic civilization, some of which have just been enumerated. It would be an enormous task to which many qualified people would have to address themselves. Some of the already existing traditional works[3] have laid the foundations in expounding the most fundamental doctrines and teachings of Sufism. But much still remains to be done in order to reveal Sufism not only in its essence but also in all its glorious manifestations and applications so that qualified people of different aptitudes and natures can all benefit spiritually from this vast ocean of grace.

The present book sets out to be no more than a humble addition to the literature on Sufism, dealing with different questions of importance to the understanding of Sufism but without attempting to give even a brief systematic exposition of all the various aspects that it comprises.[4] In the first part of the book several studies are devoted to the principal aspects of Sufism itself. In the second some of the problems of the history of Islam and of Sufism are considered, and in the third part three essays are devoted to some of the major contemporary problems faced by the modern world in general and the Muslim world in particular, problems whose solutions reside in the understanding and application of the principles of Sufism as a whole.

The essays assembled in this book (except chapter V which has never been printed before and chapter X which is to appear in a collection in Japan) appeared originally as articles over the past ten years in the following journals: *Milla wa Milla* (Melbourne), *The Journal of the Regional Cultural Institute* (Tehran), *Iran* (London), *Studies in Comparative Religion* (London), *Religious Studies* (Cambridge, England) and *The Islamic Quarterly* (London). Thanks are due to the editors of these journals for their kind permission to reproduce these articles. All the essays have been revised and in certain cases augmented.

The transliteration system employed is that followed by the new

[3] The works which have expounded with lucidity and authenticity the major facets of Sufism in European languages from the Sufi point of view include F. Schuon, *Understanding Islam*, trans. by D. M. Matheson, London, 1963 and *Dimensions of Islam*, trans. by P. Townsend, London, 1970; T. Burckhardt, *An Introduction to Sufi Doctrine*, trans. by D. M. Matheson, Lahore, 1959; M. Lings, *A Moslem Saint of the Twentieth Century*, London, 1960: L. Schaya, *La doctrine soufique de l'unité*, Paris, 1962. See also S. H. Nasr, *Three Muslim Sages*, Cambridge (Mass.), 1964, *Islamic Studies*, Beirut, 1967 and *Ideals and Realities of Islam*, London, 1966.

[4] We hope to give a more systematic treatment of Sufism in our forthcoming work on Sufism in the *Islamic Surveys* series edited by Prof. W. Montgomery Watt.

Encyclopedia of Islam, with the following exceptions: q for ḳ, j for dj, ah for final a (tâ' marbûṭah); lines are not employed to indicate when two Latin letters are the transliteration of one Arabic letter (i.e. sh for sh, kh for kh, dh for dh etc.).

The author wishes to express his gratitude to Mr William Chittick for helping with the preparation of the manuscript and to Miss Parvin Peerwani for typing it.

Our hope is that through these humble studies certain keys will be provided to open some of the doors to the treasure-house of Sufism and that other individuals will be incited to pursue serious study and research in a field which cannot but yield rich returns both spiritually and intellectually for anyone whose intentions are serious and pure. *Wa mâ tawfîqî illâ bi'llâh.*

S.H.N.
Tehran, 1970

PART I

I

Sufism and the Perennity of the Mystical Quest[1]

لقد خلقنا الانسان في احسن تقويم   ثم رددناه اسفل سافلين

Surely We created man of the best stature (*aḥsan taqwîm*)
Then We reduced him to the lowest of the low (*asfal sâfilîn*).
(Quran, XCV, 4–5; Pickthall translation)

گمان مکن که چو تو بگذری جهان گذرد   هزار شمع بکشتند وانجمن باقي است

Think not that if thou passest away, the world will also be gone;
A thousand candles have burned out, yet the circle of the Sufis remains.

The Quranic verse cited above defines the situation of man in this world in a manner that is at once perennial and universal. Man was created in the best stature (*aḥsan taqwîm*) but then fell into the terrestial condition of separation and withdrawal from his divine prototype, a condition which the Quran calls the lowest of the low (*asfal sâfilîn*). And inasmuch as the situation described in this Quranic verse pertains to the innermost nature of man it is a permanent reality that he carries within himself. No amount of supposed evolution and change can destroy the divine image which is his origin or the state of separation and hence wretchedness and misery in which he finds himself due to this very separation from his spiritual origin. Man carries both the image of perfection and the experiential certainty of separation within himself and these elements remain as permanent aspects and conditions of the human state above and beyond all historical change and transformation.[2]

[1] Originally the Charles Strong Memorial Lecture in Comparative Religion delivered in Australian Universities in 1970.

[2] After over a century of complete surrender to historicism and evolutionism only recently have some of the scholars and scientists in the West been becoming aware that the permanent elements of human nature and of the relation of man to the cosmos dominate over the transient and passing elements; hitherto these had been emphasized so much as to obliterate the much more blinding reality of the permanence of things. See E. Zolla (ed.), *I Valori permanenti nel divenire storico*, Roma, 1968, and the article in that volume by S. H. Nasr, 'Man in the Universe, Permanence amidst apparent Change', which also appears as Chapter VI of the present work.

Concerning the Quranic term *aḥsan taqwîm* the ninth/fifteenth century Sufi commentator, Kamâl al-Dîn Ḥusayn Kâshifî, writes that it means God 'created man as the most complete and perfect theophany, the most universal and all-embracing theatre of divine hierophany, so that he may become the bearer of the divine trust (*amânah*) and the source of unlimited effusion'.[3] And he identifies *asfal sâfilîn* with the world of natural passions and heedlessness. Hence man bears at once the imprint of the 'divine form'—he possesses a theomorphic nature according to the *ḥadîth*, 'God created man in His own image' (*khalaqa'Llâh âdam 'alâ ṣûratihi*)[4]—and has fallen from this innate perfection which yet he cannot forget.

The grandeur of the human state, its great possibilities and perils, and the permanent nature of man's quest after the Divine thus lies in the very fibres of human existence. Were man to be only 'of the best stature' and were he to remain in the paradisial state of proximity to the Divine and of identity with his celestial archetype, there would be no mystical[5] quest in the usual meaning of the term. There would already be union; the goal which stands at the end of the mystical and spiritual life would have already been achieved. Likewise, if man were to be only a creature of the sensory world, bound to passionate impulses and imprisoned by his natural and physical inclinations, or in other words were he to belong only to the state of *asfal sâfilîn*, again there would be no mystical quest possible. Man would not remain dissatisfied with the finite and would not continue to seek, albeit often

[3] Kamâl al-Dîn Ḥusayn Wâ'iẓ Kâshifî, *Mawâhib 'aliyyah* or *Tafsîr-i ḥusaynî*, vol. IV, Tehran, 1329 (A. H. Solar), p. 427.

[4] See F. Schoun, *Understanding Islam*, chapter I.

[5] The reader needs to be warned concerning the word 'mystical', which is used here in its original sense of having to do with the 'divine mysteries'; in other words, with a knowledge combined with love that, far from being irrational, is concerned with the intellect in its original sense, the source of reason which through its effusion illuminates the human mind and endows it with the knowledge of the spiritual order. Thus, mysticism refers to the inner aspect of a revealed and orthodox religion, bound to spiritual methods and techniques derived from that revelation, and not to vague reveries or individualistic whims and fancies or worst of all to forms of pseudo-occultism divorced from the religious context such as are becoming so prevalent in the West today. In this connection it must be specially emphasized that Sufism cannot be practiced outside of Islam even if self-styled 'masters' in the West using the name of Sufism say otherwise.

'Scientific works commonly define Ṣufism as "Moslem mysticism" and we too would readily adopt the epithet "mystical" to designate that which distinguishes Ṣufism from the simply religious aspect of Islam if that word still bore the meaning given it by the Greek Fathers of the early Christian Church and those who followed their spiritual line; they used it to designate what is related to knowledge of the "mysteries".' T. Burckhardt, *An Introduction to Sufi Doctrine*, p. 12.

blindly, the Infinite Reality which can deliver him from the bonds of the finite and the limited. He would be content as an earthly creature. Transcendence would have no meaning for him. He would be limited like other earthly creatures and also like them he would remain unaware of the fact that he is limited and bound in space and time. But precisely because both of these elements, the theomorphic nature and the terrestial crust which covers and hides this spiritual core, are parts of human nature, man lives in this world and is yet bound by his own nature to transcend it. Religion in general and the mystical quest in particular are as permanent as human existence itself, for man cannot remain man without seeking the Infinite and without wanting to transcend himself. To be human means to want to transcend the merely human. Hence to be satisfied with the merely human is to fall into the infra-human state. The history of Western man during the past five centuries provides ample proof of this contention.

The mystical quest is perennial because it lies in the nature of things, and normal human society is one in which such a quest is given recognition in the life of the collectivity. When a collectivity or society ceases to recognize this profound need and when fewer men follow the vocation of traveller upon the mystical path, then that society crumbles through the sheer weight of its own structure or dissolves as a result of psychic maladies it is not able to cure, by the very fact that it has denied to its members the only food that can satisfy the hunger of the psyche for the Spirit. In such cases certain men will still continue to seek and to follow the mystical way, but society itself will no longer be able to benefit fully from the illuminative presence of those who by the very fact of their seeking the supra-human allow their fellow men to remain at least on the human level and provide society itself with the only true criteria of its own worth and value.

If men of a spiritual and contemplative nature continue to appear even in the darkest periods of spiritual eclipse it is precisely because the economy of a human collectivity necessitates their existence. Were human society to be without any contemplatives at all, it would simply cease to exist. All terrestial existence comes from Being, the luminous source of all that exists, and being and knowledge are ultimately one. Were the light which the contemplative casts upon the terrestial environment to come to an end, the bond between Being and its earthly manifestations would terminate and the latter would become deprived of the conscious ontological nexus with its source. It would fall into the abyss of nothingness. The tradition according to which the world will not come to an end as long as there are men on earth who invoke the name of God refers to the same truth, for the invocation of the Divine Name is the royal path towards spiritual realization in Sufism. Moreover, since the purpose of creation is that through it, as summarized in the heart of the gnostic (*al-'ârif bi'Llâh*), the Divine comes to know Itself, but for the presence in the world of contemplative man the creation itself would cease to have a reason for existing.[6] That is why in Islam it is said 'The earth shall never be empty of the "witness of God" ' (*Lâ takhlu'l-arḍ 'an ḥujjat Allâh*). The quest after the infinite alone provides meaning for the finite world in which man finds himself on earth. The imprint of that perfection which man bears within himself makes any finite existence bearable for man only provided it can lead him to the Infinite and the Absolute.[7] Hence the perennity of the mystical quest and the striving of man throughout the ages to see beyond the finite the Infinite Reality which determines and encompasses all things.

The cosmos itself continually reveals to man the eternal message of the Truth. Its finite forms reveal the Traces of the Infinite. As 'Alî said, 'I wonder at the man who observes the Universe created by God and doubts His Being.'[8] But to gain this awareness man has need of revelation, which like the cosmos comes from the Infinite and the Absolute but in a more direct sense, and hence serves as the key for the unfolding of the mysteries of man's own being as well as those of the Universe. Revelation is in itself a gift that has descended from the Divine Mercy (*al-raḥmah*) to enable man to pass beyond the finite to the Infinite. Having fallen from the state of 'the best stature' to that of the 'lowest of the low' man cannot regain the former state save through the grace of heaven. It is only by virtue of the beatific vision that he is able to see the cosmos as reflections of aspects of the spiritual world in the mirror of the material and the temporal.

[6] The metaphysical principle that knowledge and being are ultimately one, and that through intellection the cosmos has gained its existence, underlies both the gnostic and the theosophical doctrines of Islam. Without an understanding of this principle the essential role that gnosis and contemplation of the Divine play in the sustenance of the cosmic environment cannot be understood. For an explanation of this principle see S. H. Nasr, *Science and Civilization in Islam*, chapter 13 and *An Introduction to Islamic Cosmological Doctrines*, Cambridge (U.S.A.), 1964, chapters XI on.

[7] 'Man, whether he be concerned in the plural or the singular, or whether his function be direct or indirect, stands like "a fragment of absoluteness" and is made for the Absolute; he has no other choice before him. In any case, one can define the social in terms of Truth, but one cannot define Truth in terms of the social.' F. Schuon, 'No Activity Without Truth', *Studies in Comparative Religion*, Autumn, 1969, p. 196.

[8] *Nahj al-balâghah*, trans. by Syed Mohammed Askari Jafery, Karachi, 1960, p. 286.

بنزد آنکه جانش در تجلّی است　　همه عالم کتاب حقّ تعالی است

عرض اعراب وجوهر چون حروفست　　مراتب همچو آیات وقوفست

To him, whose soul attains the beatific vision,
The universe is the book of 'The Truth Most High'.
Accidents are its vowels, and substance its consonants,
And grades of creatures its verses and pauses.[9]
(Shaykh Maḥmûd Shabistarî)

The saving grace of revelation alone makes possible this journey of the soul from the outward to the inward, from the periphery to the Centre, from the form to the meaning, the journey which is none other than the mystical quest itself. And because of the intimate relation the soul possesses with the cosmos, this journey is at once a penetration to the centre of the soul and a migration to the abode beyond the cosmos. In both places, which are in reality but a single locus, resides the Divine Presence, the Presence which is at once completely our-Self and totally other than ourselves.

As a Sufi master of the last century has written: 'The soul is an immense thing; it is the whole cosmos, since it is the copy of it. Everything which is in the cosmos is to be found in the soul; equally everything in the soul is in the cosmos. Because of this fact, he who masters his soul most certainly masters the cosmos, just as he who is dominated by his soul is certainly dominated by the whole cosmos.'[10]

It is only by the grace of revelation or the message from Heaven in whatever form it has been revealed within the different religions of mankind, that the soul is able to free itself from the taint of finitude and imperfection to seek the Infinite and to pursue the task for which it was created. To quote Khayyam.

O soul; from earthly taint when purified,
As spirit free, thou shalt toward heaven ride,
Thy home the empyrean: Shame on thee
Who dost in this clay tenement reside:

In love eternal He created me
And first He taught the lore of charity.
Then from my heart he filed a key that might
Unlock the treasure of Reality.

[9] Sa'd ud Dîn Maḥmûd Shabistarî, *Gulshan-i Râz, The Mystic Rose Garden*, trans. by E. H. Whinfield, London, 1880, p. 21.

[10] Shaykh al-'Arabî al-Darqâwî, *Letters of a Sufi Master*, trans. by T. Burckhardt, London, 1969, p. 4.

In some low Inn I'd rather seek Thy face,
Than pray without Thee toward the Niche's place.
O First and Last of all: As Thou dost will,
Burn me in Hell—or save me by Thy grace![11]

But the saving grace of revelation is always there and has always been there. To be human is to see before man the path that leads from the relative to the Absolute; it is to be able to follow the mystical way. As Rûmî says,

The moment thou to this low world wast given,
A ladder stood whereby thou mightest aspire.[12]

The transparency of the cosmos and its function as a ladder to the Metacosmic Reality can only be realized if the grace provided by revelation is operative and if by virtue of this grace the soul has been able to penetrate into its centre and truly become itself.[13] And this possibility is always there even if it is not realized by all men. Both revelation and the cosmos—the second by virtue of the first—can lead men to that Infinite whose joy and beatitude so many vainly seek in the shadows of the finite world.

Revelation is limited in its outer form; it is outwardly finite and so appears to men in its rites, doctrines and symbols as one more set of finite forms along with others that surround him in this world. But unlike other forms, the religious and revealed forms open inwardly toward the Infinite, because it is from the supra-formal Centre that they originate, the Centre which contains all these forms and is yet above them.[14] The reason for the persistence of traditional forms and symbols is none other than this fact that although outwardly they are forms subject to time and space, their inner content leads to the Infinite. Hence they reflect even in the transient world of time and space the permanence that belongs to the spiritual world. They thus fulfil that perennial need of man to transcend the finite, to go beyond the transient and seek the permanent.

[11] From the quatrains translated by E. H. Rodwell, cited in M. Smith, *The Sufi Path of Love, An Anthology of Sufism*, London, 1954, p. 63.

[12] Rûmî, *Dîwâni Shams Tabrîz*, trans. by R. A. Nicholson, Cambridge, 1898, p. 343.

[13] On this question see S. H. Nasr, *Science and Civilization in Islam*, Chapter 13 and *An Introduction to Islamic Cosmological Doctrines*, chapter XV.

[14] This cardinal truth has been fully explained in the different writings of F. Schuon, especially his *Transcendent Unity of Religions*, trans. by P. Townsend, London, 1953.

As for the cosmos, traditional cosmologies both Islamic and Christian and even those of some of the Hindu and Buddhist schools—to speak only of some of the better known examples—have depicted it as finite in outward form, but these cosmologies, like revelation or tradition to which they are intimately bound, are infinite in their symbolical content. The traditional cosmos is bound in space; its limits are almost 'felt' and certainly visible. When traditional man looked to the stars he saw in the heaven of the fixed stars the limits of the Universe. Beyond that heaven there was no 'space' or 'matter' (*lâ khala' wa lâ mala'* as the Islamic philosophers would say) but only the Divine Presence. This finite cosmos, however, was far from being a prison without an opening. On the contrary by the very fact of its finite form it served as an icon to be contemplated and transcended. Thanks to its symbolism—the concentric spheres acting as a most powerful and efficient symbol for the states of being which man must traverse to reach Being Itself—the content of this cosmos was infinite and its finite forms like the forms of religion led man to an inner content which was limitless.

Modern science since Giordano Bruno has broken the boundaries of the cosmos and hence destroyed the very notion of 'cosmos', which means literally 'order'. The Universe has become limitless outwardly. But precisely due to the lack of a 'metaphysics or theology of nature' in the West, the symbolic meaning of this new vision of the Universe has not been made generally known, and moreover, because modern science leaves aside the symbolic significance of things, the content of this outwardly 'infinite' Universe remains finite. It is bound to the purely material level of existence. In a sense the situation has become the reverse of what existed in the traditional sciences. There, the cosmos is outwardly finite but with an inner content that leads to the Infinite, whereas in modern science the Universe is outwardly 'infinite' but inwardly finite. Hence on the one hand modern man seeks to fly to the planets and 'conquer space', due to an unconscious urge or 'mystique' to transcend his earthly finitude—but in a physical manner which is the only manner modern men believe to be possible—and on the other hand those modern men who understand the full implication of the finiteness of the contents of the Universe as conceived by modern science are subdued by this very realization and often seek an outlet from the tyranny of the finite physical world through the use of drugs, which they believe will open to them 'the doors of perception' into another world.

Both those who wish to fly into space and those who would break the hold of physical sensations upon them by the use of drugs enabling them to experience reality differently prove through these very efforts the perennity of the need for spiritual experience and of the necessity to follow the mystical quest, in the sense that man in whatever age he lives needs the Infinite and the Absolute in order to remain man. His finite psyche can remain sound and healthy only when it is in quest of that Beloved the union with whom is the goal of all mystical romances.

The failure of such efforts, whether they be space flights or 'trips' made possible through drugs—a failure instinctively felt by most men to be a poor substitute for that felicity and peace which accompanies all true contacts with the Spirit—itself proves that only a true mysticism that comes from God through one of His revealed religions can render the mystical quest successful. Only a path that comes from God can lead to Him and only such a path can guarantee the soul's final beatitude and union with the One. Only traditional authority can protect the soul from the great dangers that lurk upon the path of him who wishes to climb mountains without a guide and without following an existing trail. The end of the one path, of true mysticism, is the absorption of the soul in its divine prototype; the end of the other, the pseudo-mysticism so rampant today, is the dissolution and decomposition of the very substance of the soul. The soul of man was made by God and only He has the right to remould it. He has given man the urge for the mystical life and the desire for the perfection which lies at the end of the path. He has also provided for man the genuine means to reach this end. It is for man to choose the path which will lead him from the *asfal sâfilîn* to the state of *aḥsan taqwîm*, the path which will allow him to be truly himself.

Sufism is one such path, placed by God within the bosom of Islam in order to provide the possibility of spiritual realization for the millions of men who over the ages have followed and continue to follow the religion of the Quran. In its essence it joins the paths of spiritual realization found in other traditions while in its formal aspect it shares the genius and the particular features of Islam.[15] It is the path within Islam that leads from the particular to the Universal, from multiplicity to Unity, from form to the supra-formal Essence. Its function is to enable man to realize Divine Unity (*al-tawḥîd*), the truth which has always been and will always be. It is the depository of the 'eternal mysteries' (*asrâr-i alast*) going back to the primordial covenant made between God and man even before the creation of the

[15] In fact, as already mentioned, the Sufis refer to all true spiritual paths and metaphysical doctrines of other religions as *taṣawwuf.*

world.[16] Its message is therefore perennial, referring to the profound nature of man which lies beneath the layers of dross that the passage of the ages and the gradual removal of man from his original perfection in the state of *aḥsan taqwîm* have imposed upon that original theomorphic kernel at the centre of man's being. In its doctrines Sufism speaks of a truth that is at once perennial and universal; in its methods it employs techniques which are conformable to the nature of the men of this age, a nature which in its essence remains unchanged from that of primordial man but which in its accidents and outward manifestations has become ever more impermeable to spiritual influences and which in its contemplative faculties has become ever more atrophied and weakened.

Sufism serves essentially the function of reminding man of who he really is, which means that man is awakened from this dream which he calls his ordinary life and that his soul is freed from the confines of that illusory prison of the ego which has its objective counterpart in what is called 'the world' in religious parlance. By appealing to the true nature of man, Sufism fulfils the real needs of his nature, not what he feels to be his needs in terms of outer impressions and forms which the soul receives continually from the outer world into which it has plunged its roots. Man seeks his psychic and spiritual needs outwardly precisely because he does not know who he is. Sufism reminds man to seek all that he needs inwardly within himself, to tear his roots from the outer world and plunge them in the Divine Nature, which resides at the centre of his heart. Sufism removes man from his lowly state of *asfal sâfilîn* in order to reinstate him in his primordial perfection of *aḥsan taqwîm* wherein he finds within himself all that he had sought outwardly, for being united with God he is separate from nothing. As Ḥâfiẓ says,

سالها دل طلب جام جم از ما می کرد وآنچه خود داشت ز بیگانه تمنّی می کرد

For many years our heart sought the 'cup of Jamshîd'[17] from us;
It sought from the stranger what it possessed itself.[18]

[16] The term *alast* refers to the Quranic verse *Alastu bi rabbikum*. 'Am I not your Lord?' (VII, 172), which concerns the relation between God and man in pre-eternity before the creation of the world. See S. H. Nasr, *Ideals and Realities of Islam*, pp. 24 ff.

[17] The *Jâm-i jam*, or 'cup of Jamshîd,' refers to the cup of the mythical Persian king Jamshîd in which he saw the reflection of all events and phenomena. In Sufism it has become the symbol of the heart of the gnostic in which all realities are reflected, the eye of the heart (*'ayn al-qalb* in Arabic or *chasm-i dil* in Persian) with which the mystic 'sees' the supernal realities.

[18] Translation by S. H. Nasr.

To discover the 'cup of Jamshîd' within, one must sacrifice the carnal self which hides from man the Spirit dwelling within him. As Abû Yazîd Basṭâmî has said. 'I triply divorced the world and alone proceeded to the Alone. I stood before the Presence and cried, "Lord God, I desire none but Thee. If I possess Thee, I possess all."

'When God recognized my sincerity, the first grace that He accorded me was that he removed the chaff of the self from before me.'[19]

Sufism speaks essentially of three elements: the nature of God, the nature of man and the spiritual virtues, which alone make possible the realization of God and which alone can prepare man to become worthy of the exalted station of *aḥsan taqwîm*, of becoming the total theophany of God's Names and Qualities.[20] These are the eternal elements of Sufism as of every true mystical path. The end is God, the beginning is man in his terrestial state and the way or path is that which links man to God, that is, it is the method that engenders the spiritual virtues in the soul of man and the doctrine that outlines the contour of the Universe through which the traveller or mystic is to journey to reach the Divine Presence and gain true immortality.

The heart enquired of the soul
What is the beginning of this business?
What its end, and what its fruit?
The soul answered:
The beginning of it is
the annihilation of self,
Its end faithfulness,
And its fruit immortality.[21]
(Khwâjah 'Abdullâh Anṣârî)

The mystic path as it exists in Sufism is one in which man dies to his carnal nature in order to be reborn *in divinis* and hence to become united with the Truth.

Will the seeker of God be content to be far?
Nay, for he needeth no less than Union. . . .

[19] Farîd al-Dîn 'Aṭṭâr, *Muslim Saints and Mystics*, trans. by A. J. Arberry London, 1966, p. 122.

[20] See F. Schuon, *Understanding Islam*, pp. 131 ff. Concerning Sufism see also Schuon, *Dimensions of Islam*; T. Burckhardt, *An Introduction to Sufi Doctrine*; M. Lings, *A Moslem Saint of the Twentieth Century*; S. H. Nasr, *Three Muslim Sages*, chapter III; and S. H. Nasr, *Islamic Studies*, Part III.

[21] Translated by Sir Jogendra Singh, *The Invocations of Sheikh 'Abdullâh Ansâri*, London, Wisdom of the East Series, 1939, p. 42.

He dieth before his death to live in his Lord,
Since after this death is the supreme migration.
He calleth himself to account ere he be called,
He herein most fitted to act for the Truth.
The Truth's Being he seeth before his own,
And after it, and wheresoever he turn.
Alone God was, and with Him naught else.
He is now as He was, lastly as firstly,
Essentially One, with naught beside Himself,
Inwardly Hidden, Outwardly Manifest,
Without beginning, without end. Whate'er thou seest,
Seest thou His Being. Absolute Oneness
No 'but' hath and no 'except'. How should God's Essence
Be confined with a veil? No veil there but His Light.[22]

(Shaykh al-'Alawî)

What Sufism has to teach about the Divine Nature, the Universe and man, comprising nearly the whole of Sufi doctrine, cannot be analyzed here. We can only emphasize that the Sufi teachings revolve around the two fundamental doctrines of the 'Transcendent Unity of Being' (*waḥdat al-wujûd*) and the Universal or Perfect Man (*al-insân al-kâmil*).[23] All things are theophanies of the Divine Names and Qualities and derive their existence from the One Being who alone 'is'. And man is the only creature in this world who is centrally and axially located so that he reflects the Divine Names and Qualities in a total and conscious manner. To become a saint in Islam is to realize all the possibilities of the human state, to become the Universal Man. The mystical quest is none other than the realization of this state, which is also union with God, for the Universal Man is the mirror in which are reflected all the Divine Names and Qualities. Through the Universal Man God contemplates Himself and all things that He has brought into being.

The message of Sufism is timeless precisely because it speaks of truths which determine what one might call the pre-temporal existence of man in relation with God and which are based on elements of reality both transcendent and immanent within human nature which neither evolve nor decay. To this doctrinal message is attached a method derived like the doctrine from the Quran and prophetic *Ḥadîth* and possessing efficacy only by virtue of the particular grace

[22] Lings, *A Moslem Saint of the Twentieth Century*, pp. 199–200.
[23] See S. H. Nasr, *Science and Civilization in Islam*, chapter 13.

(*barakah*) made available through initiation and transmitted from master to disciple going back to the Prophet himself.

To understand the doctrine is to possess intellectual intuition (*dhawq*), which is already a divine gift. But to accept to follow the method, to realize its necessity and to be willing to surrender oneself to the discipline of a Master as well as to the obligations of the *Sharî'ah* or Divine Law, which is the basis for all authentic practices of Sufism, requires yet another divine gift, which is none other than faith (*îmân*).

'The merit of faith is fidelity to the supernaturally natural receptivity of primordial man; it means remaining as God made us and remaining at His disposition with regard to a message from Heaven which might be contrary to earthly experience, while being incontestable in view of subjective as well as objective criteria.'[24]

If man possesses this faith and is willing to undergo the necessary spiritual travail under the direction of an authentic Master, then he is reborn in the spiritual world with its infinite horizons and delivered from the prison of contingency and the finiteness of the terrestial world that surrounds him. Sufism, based upon the sacred forms of Islam, enables man to transcend the finite and reach the Infinite through these very forms. Thanks to the *barakah* present in its methods, it makes possible the liquefaction of the outer crust of man's being, thus revealing to man his own divine centre, which is the 'Throne of the Compassionate' (*'arsh al-raḥmân*) to use the language of the *ḥadîth*, and by virtue of the same transformation making the cosmos and all that it contains transparent so that the infinite content becomes revealed through the finite form. In this manner Sufism achieves the goal of the mystical quest, a goal which is perennially sought since, as already explained, it lies within the depth of human existence itself. As long as man is man this search continues and must continue; otherwise the world would simply cease to exist, for it would no longer have an empowering reason to continue. To quote Ḥâfiẓ again,

تا زمیخانه و می نام ونشان خواهد بود   سرما خاك ره پیر مغان خواهد بود
حلقهٔ پیر مغان از ازلم در گوش است   برهمانیم که بودیم وهمان خواهد بود

As long as the name and sign of the tavern and the wine remain
Our head shall be the dust of the path of the 'Wise Magi'.
The ring of the 'Wise Magi' has been in my ear since pre-eternity;

[24] F. Schuon, 'Understanding and Believing', *Studies in Comparative Religion*, Summer 1969, p. 131.

We continue to be what we were, and we will continue to be so
in the future.[25]

With its universal doctrine and method as well as the living tradition which guarantees the efficacy of its practices, Sufism contains within itself the possibility of being practised in any circumstance in which man finds himself, in the traditional world as well as in the modern one whose manifestations seem in so many ways to negate the Divine and to make man forget who he is and where he is going. Since it is based on the social and juridical teachings of Islam, Sufism is meant to be practised within society and not in a monastic environment outside the social order. But the attitudes of monastic life are integrated with the daily life lived within the human community. The Sufi bears spiritual poverty (*faqr*) within himself even if he lives outwardly amidst the riches of the world. Sufism is in fact often called 'Muḥammadan poverty' (*al-faqr al-muḥammadī*). The world has died in the Sufi and he lives in the world without being seduced by it. Sufism is able to integrate man into his Divine Centre wherever he may happen to be, provided he is willing to dedicate himself to the Way, which, being sacred, asks of man all that he is.[26] Likewise Sufism is the way of integration of the active and contemplative lives so that man is able to remain receptive inwardly to the influences of heaven and lead an intense inner contemplative life while outwardly remaining most active in a world which he moulds according to his inner spiritual nature, instead of becoming its prisoner as happens to the profane man. Men without spiritual principles may claim to make the world about them and to create their own 'times'. Actually it is their times that make them. Only the spiritual man makes his times and moulds the environment about him according to the principles that dominate him inwardly.

Through this possibility of interiorization Sufism bestows upon Islam a dimension in depth through which outer forms become channels of an inner illumination. Through it the exoteric forms of Islam gain the universality which comes from the Formless alone. It also regenerates the moral teachings of the religion from within and at the same time provides those metaphysical and cosmological doctrines which alone can answer the needs for causality on the part

[25] Translated by S. H. Nasr. Wine, which combines of the nature of water and fire, symbolizes in Sufi imagery both divine love and the realized aspect of gnosis, while the tavern is the spiritual centre of the Sufis. The term 'Wise Magi' (*pîr-i mughân*) of course symbolizes the spiritual master.

[26] See chapter II.

of certain types of believers and prevent the intelligent from seeking the fulfilment of these needs outside the tradition.

Sufism also renders a great service to Islam in clarifying the question of comparative religion which, because of the spread of modernism, is becoming an important problem for certain Muslims and will certainly become even more important in the future. Religions can be studied historically as phenomena or theologically as dogmatic systems or can even be tolerated for humanitarian reasons. But this is far from enough. To tolerate another religion is to believe it to be false yet accept its presence, much as one tolerates pain as inevitable but would rather that it did not exist. To understand another orthodox religion in depth is not simply to analyse its historical manifestations or even its theological formulations and then to tolerate them; rather is it to reach, at least by intellectual anticipation, the inner truths from which spring all the outer manifestations of a tradition. It means to be able to go from the phenomena of a religion to the noumena, from the forms to the essences wherein resides the truth of all religions and where alone a religion can be really understood and accepted.

Being itself the message of the essence in the form or of the Centre at the periphery, Sufism can guide man from the phenomena to the noumena, from the form (*ṣûrah*) to the meaning (*ma'nâ*) to use the Sufi technical terminology itself. This fact coupled with the universal character of Islam, as reflected in the insistence of the Quran upon man's accepting the authenticity of previous religions, has made of the Sufis throughout history the great proponents of the 'transcendent unity of religions', whose principles they have explicitly formulated. Some like Ibn 'Arabî and Mawlânâ Jalâl al-Dîn Rûmî have even applied this concept to specific teachings of non-Islamic religions. Sufism provides the metaphysics necessary to carry out the study of comparative religion in depth so that man can accept the validity of every detail of the authentic religions of mankind and at the same time see beyond these details to the transcendent unity of these religions.[27] It is the treasury from which Islam can draw in its confrontation with other religions of the world in the contemporary context. It can also provide many principles for Western scholars who are seeking so desperately today for a meaningful study of comparative religion which would do justice to the nature of religion itself.[28]

[27] See F. Schuon, *Transcendent Unity of Religions* and Chapter IX of the present work.

[28] The efforts of W. C. Smith in several of his recent works and of K. Morgan and Huston Smith come to mind particularly in this context.

There are also other fields in which Sufism could be of operative and practical significance for the West, even among those who cannot follow it themselves. Being a living example of the mystical way in its fullness, it contains universal teachings which could certainly help resuscitate forgotten elements in the Christian mystical life, elements which alone can revitalize the metaphysical and mystical teachings and methods of Christianity,[29] of which there is such a desperate need today. Unfortunately until now most Western scholars dealing with Sufism have tried to explain it away in terms of historical influences as if the yearning of man's soul for God could ever be due to historical borrowing. But now, thanks to the few authentic and authoritative works on Sufism which have appeared during the past few years,[30] those whose interests are serious are becoming ever more aware of the aid that Sufism can offer them in charting a course toward the Centre across this web of illusion and confusion which the modern world has spun around the minds and souls of so many men. Because it is concerned with the perennial and the universal, Sufism remains as relevant today as in every past age; it speaks to the seeking non-Muslim as well as to the Muslim, provided there is an ear to hear and an eye to see.

Granted that Sufism can provide answers for the perennial questions posed for man by the very nature of his situation in the world and of his own intelligence, that is, questions concerning the mysteries of 'pre-natal' and 'posthumous' existence and of our present situation in the total order of things, what about the pressing and urgent problems of modern man? The answer is that had not the truths expounded by Sufism, as by every other authentic metaphysical teaching, been forgotten by the modern world, there would not have been the so-called pressing problems of modern man. Problems always result from a particular ignorance. Modern man wants to eliminate the transcendent dimension of his life and yet not suffer from suffocation in the two-dimensional world he has created for himself. He wants to kill all the gods and yet remain human, which is a contradiction and an impossibility precisely because, as stated

[29] Despite the fact that he still had much to learn in questions of the authentic initiatic life and especially of the metaphysical doctrines that underly it, Thomas Merton sought genuine contacts with Sufism until the very end of his life, in the hope of revitalizing by this means the contemplative methods in Christianity. Massignon, the great French specialist in Sufism, also drew on Sufism as a practical aid to his Christian spiritual life.

[30] One has in mind particularly the writings of F. Schuon, T. Burckhardt, M. Lings and several other of the traditional authors in the West. Some of these works have been referred to in previous notes.

above, man can remain human only by being faithful to his own theomorphic nature.

To the problems caused by the forgetting of the transcendent dimension of life by modern man, by the imprisonment of his being in the cage of the material world and by the limiting of his horizon to a purely corporeal one (even if this contains nebulae millions of light years distant from us), Sufism would answer by recalling the truth that man was made for immortality and his intelligence was created to grasp the Absolute. Hence no mortal existence, no matter how streamlined, can satisfy his soul, nor can all the information in the world, with which he is bombarded day and night, take the place of the Absolute which his intelligence seeks in virtue of its own nature. To the problems of the pathetic lot of modern, secularized man, Sufism would answer by pointing out that man has become miserable only because he no longer knows who he is; and the modern sciences of man as they are usually taught do not aid him one iota in discovering his true identity.[31] It would add further that the very quest of youth today for 'vision' through drugs, or for occultist and pseudo-mystical practices is itself proof in reverse of the Sufi conception of human nature. The positivists of the nineteenth century certainly did not extrapolate such happenings as we see today to be the next stage in the so-called 'progress' of man. They never thought that in the most 'progressive' countries in the middle of the twentieth century there would be interest in everything from Yoga to alchemy. They never guessed that man could not remain satisfied for long with the 'positivist' conception of reality into which he had been forced, as into a strait-jacket, by the fathers of positivism and scientism. Sufism sees in all the efforts made by so many today to escape the prison of material existence a desperate attempt—since for them the false idols such as 'progress' and 'evolution' have been broken—to reach the Infinite and the Eternal; an attempt which, alas, because of the lack of discrimination and discipline as well as the scarcity of available mystical ways of a genuine nature, results often in a fall into the infernal depths of the psyche instead of a rising into the state of beatific vision. But these distressing phenomena still remain a proof, albeit in reverse, of the perennity of the mystical quest.

On the positive side the very doctrines and methods of Sufism can act as criteria for judging all that passes in the modern world for 'ways of realization', at least for those with a discerning spirit. It can also

[31] See J. Servier, *L'Homme et l'invisible*, Paris, 1964, where the author, himself an anthropologist, analyzes with much insight the shortcomings which prevent modern anthropology from understanding who the 'anthropos' really is.

turn this urge to follow the mystical way into a wholesome and meaningful direction for those who are willing to accept its discipline or to apply its insights to their own situation. In both cases, Sufism remains a grace from Heaven and a sign of Divine Mercy (*raḥmah*) not only for Muslims but also for non-Muslims, some of whom are seeking so desperately, and so often in the wrong places. In such cases Sufism can act as the net that prevents a fall into the bottomless pit of the 'inferior waters'.

The presence of Sufism in the world is thus a sign of both the perennial character of the mystical quest and the eternal effusion of the Divine Mercy. It is a reminder of the eternal covenant made between God and man by virtue of which man remains in quest of the Divinity as long as he remains truly human. The man who remembers this pact and his own true identity remains ever faithful to his nature, hence faithful to his quest for the Divinity, for that Divinity which is already present at the centre of his being.

هرگزم نقش تو از لوح دل وجان نرود   هرگز از یاد من آن سرو خرامان نرود
از دماغ من سرگشته خیال دهنت   بجفای فلك وغصّه دوران نرود
در ازل بست دلم با سرزلفت پیوند   تا ابد سر نکشد وز سرپیمان نرود
هرچه جز بار غمت بردل مسکین منست   برود از دل من وزدل من آن نرود
آنچنان مِهرتوام دردل من جای گرفت   که اگر سر برود از دل واز جان نرود

Thy form shall never leave the tablet of my heart and soul;
That strutting cypress tree shall never leave my memory.
The thought of thy lips, from the brain of one bewildered like
  myself,
Shall never leave, whatever be the oppression of heaven or the
  grief of the age.
My heart became bound to the lock of thy hair from pre-eternity;
It will never rebel even until post-eternity; it shall never break
  its pact.
Whatever lies upon my heart, save the weight of thy sorrow,
Shall pass away, but thy sorrow shall not leave my heart.
Thy love hath become planted in my heart and soul in such a way
That were my head to disappear, thy love would still remain.[32]
(Ḥâfiẓ)

[32] Translated by S. H. Nasr.

Precisely because it is a message of the eternal to what is permanent and abiding within man, Sufism, like other authentic spiritual ways, is perennial and remains engraved in the very texture of the human soul. Men come and go but Sufism remains immutable and transcendent like the vault of heaven, reminding man of the immortality and beatitude that are his in principle and could become so in fact through Divine grace and his own spiritual effort.

II

Sufism and the Integration of Man

Islam is the religion of unity (*tawḥîd*) and all veritable aspects of Islamic doctrine and practice reflect this central and cardinal principle. The *Sharî'ah* itself is a vast network of injunctions and regulations which relate the world of multiplicity inwardly to a single Centre which conversely is reflected in the multiplicity of the circumference. In the same way Islamic art seeks always to relate the multiplicity of forms, shapes and colours to the One, to the Centre and Origin, thereby reflecting *tawḥîd* in its own way in the world of forms with which it is concerned.

Sufism, being the marrow of the bone or the inner dimension of the Islamic revelation, is the means *par excellence* whereby *tawḥîd* is achieved. All Muslims believe in Unity as expressed in the most universal sense possible by the *Shahâdah, Lâ ilâha ill'Allâh.* But it is only the Sufi, he who has realized the mysteries of *tawḥîd*, who knows what this assertion means. It is only he who sees God everywhere.

In fact the whole programme of Sufism, of the spiritual way or *Ṭarîqah*, is to free man from the prison of multiplicity, to cure him from hypocrisy and to make him whole, for it is only in being whole that man can become holy. Men confess to one God but actually live and act as if there were many gods. They thus suffer from the cardinal sin of 'polytheism' or *shirk*, from a hypocrisy whereby on one level they profess one thing and on another act according to something else. Sufism seeks to bring this *shirk* into the open and thereby to cure the soul of this deadly malady. Its aim is to make man whole again as he was in the Edenic state. In other words the goal of Sufism is the integration of man in all the depth and breadth of his existence, in all the amplitude which is included in the nature of the universal man (*al-insân al-kâmil*).

Man, being the vice-gerent of God on earth (*khalîfah*) and the theatre wherein the Divine Names and Qualities are reflected, can reach felicity only by remaining faithful to this nature or by being truly himself. And this in turn implies that he must become integrated. God is one and so man must become whole in order to become one. To be dissipated and compartmentalized, to be lost in the never-ending play of mental images and concepts, or psychic tensions and forces, is to be removed from that state of wholeness which our inner state demands of us. Many today would like to be sophisticated at all costs, even preferring to be sophisticated and enter hell rather than be simple and go to paradise; nevertheless, the state of simplicity is closer than that of sophistication to the innocence and purity which is the condition of celestial beatitude, for as Christ said we must be like children in order to enter heaven.

The end of Sufism is the attainment of this state of purity and wholeness, not through negation of intelligence, as is often the case in the kind of piety fostered by certain modern religious movements, but through the integration of each element of one's being into its own proper centre. Man is composed of body, mind and spirit and each needs to be integrated on its own level. Although the body is the most outward aspect of man, having its own objective existence and mode of action, it is not the greatest obstacle on the path of integration. The domain with which man identifies himself and in which he is most often caught up is the labyrinth of incongruent images and thoughts, or the intermediate mental plane including the psychological forces at play at this level. That is why Sufism turns first of all to the problems of this vast intermediate world that is so difficult to harness and bring under control.

Men are usually either of a contemplative or an active nature, or from another point of view they predominantly either think or make, but in modern times the balance has been tilted heavily in favour of action over contemplation, thus bringing about the disequilibrium which characterizes the modern world. Since it is meant for men of both types of spiritual capability, Sufism has provided the means whereby both groups of men can begin to integrate their mental activity. The person who is prone to thinking and learning and who wants to know the causes of things can only begin to follow a spiritual way if he is presented with a doctrine of the nature of reality, wherein different domains are interrelated and his need for causality is fulfilled. Sufi doctrine, which is precisely such a doctrine and which must be distinguished from philosophy as understood today, is not the fruit of an attempt by a particular mind to devise a closed system with which to embrace the whole of reality; it is not the objectivization of the limitations of a particular thinker as most philosophy has latterly become. In fact it is not so much the fruit of thinking as of being. It is the vision, *theoria* in its original sense and as still understood in Orthodox theology, of reality by one who has gained this vision through a new mode of existence.

Sufi doctrine is presented to the man with a bewildered mind as a theoretical knowledge of the structure of reality and of man's place in it. It is itself the fruit of the spiritual vision of seers and sages who, having achieved the state of wholeness, have been given a vision of the whole. And in turn it is the means whereby others can be led to wholeness. It thus stands at the beginning and at the end of the spiritual path. The role of doctrine in the integration of man can hardly be overemphasized, especially for modern man, who is over-cerebral, thinking too much and often wrongly. The maze of contradictory assertions, the ambiguities and intellectual snares that characterize modern thought, are the greatest obstacle to the integration of the mind and can only be cured through the purifying effect of Sufi metaphysical doctrine which washes away the dross of contingency and multiplicity. In traditional Islamic society doctrine is usually taught step by step along with practical methods to match the gradual advancement upon the path. Nor is there such an acute need for it at the beginning because the *Sharî'ah* and traditional teachings about the nature of things satisfy in most cases the needs of the mind for knowledge and of the imagination for images and forms. But in the confusion of the modern world Sufi doctrine is a *sine qua non* for the integration of man's mind and being, preparing the ground for the actual realization of the verities whose theoretical knowledge the doctrine conveys.

Sufi doctrine consists of metaphysics, cosmology, psychology and an eschatology that is often linked up with psychology and occasionally with metaphysics. The metaphysical aspect of the doctrine delineates firstly the nature of Reality, the Oneness of the Divine Essence which alone 'is' in the absolute sense and prior to which there is nothing; then the theophany of the Essence through the Divine Names and Qualities and through the determination of the different states of being; and finally the nature of man as the total theophany (*tajallî*) of the Names and Qualities. The doctrine of unity or *tawḥîd* forms the axis of all Sufi metaphysics and it is in fact the misunderstanding of this cardinal doctrine that has caused so many orientalists to accuse Sufism of pantheism. Sufi doctrine does not assert that God is the world but that the world to the degree that it is real cannot be completely other than God; were it to be so it would become a totally independent reality, a deity of its own, and would destroy the absoluteness and the Oneness that belong to God alone.

Sufi metaphysics, moreover, delineates the intermediate levels of existence between the corporeal world and God, levels of reality which Cartesian dualism removed from the world-view of modern European philosophy, leaving an impoverished picture of reality which remains to this day a formidable obstacle to the integration of contemporary man's mind and indeed of his being. The intermediate planes of existence are precisely those which relate the physical world to the purely transcendental archetypes and enable man to escape the puerile debate between idealism and realism, each of which has inherited a portion of reality as segmented and divided by the scissors of Descartes' *cogito ergo sum* and its consequent dualism.

As for cosmology, Sufi doctrine does not expound details of physics or chemistry but a total science of the cosmos through which man discovers where he is in the multiple structured cosmic reality and where he should be going. The goal of the spiritual man is to journey through the cosmos and ultimately beyond it. Sufi cosmology provides the plan with the aid of which man can get his bearings for this journey. It is a map of the Universe which he must possess if he is to pass through its dangerous pitfalls and precipices. Sufi cosmology thus deals, not with the quantitative aspects of things as is the case in modern science, but with their qualitative and symbolic aspects. It casts a light upon things so that they become worthy subjects of contemplation, lucid and transparent, losing their habitual opaqueness and darkness.

Sufism was able to integrate many medieval sciences such as Hermeticism into its perspective precisely because these sciences reflect the unicity of nature and the interrelatedness of things; inasmuch as they deal with the symbolic and qualitative nature of objects and phenomena they accord well with the perspective of Sufism. Moreover, since Sufism is based on experience (the one kind of experience which in fact modern man who boasts so much about his experimental outlook hardly ever attempts to undergo) it has found it possible to cultivate both natural and mathematical sciences in accordance with its own perspective. The history of Islamic science bears witness to many an outstanding Muslim scientist who was a Sufi. However, the primary function of Sufi cosmology and sciences of nature is to provide a prototype of the cosmos for the traveller upon the path (*sâlik*) and to demonstrate the interrelation between all things and that unicity of all cosmic existence which nature displays so vividly if only one were to take the necessary care to observe it.

As for psychology, it must be remembered that Sufism contains a complete method of curing the illnesses of the soul and in fact succeeds where so many modern psychiatric and psychoanalytical methods, with all their extravagant claims, fail. That is because only the higher can know the lower; only the spirit can know the psyche and illuminate its dark corners and crevasses. Only he whose soul has become integrated and illuminated has the right and the wherewithal to cure the souls of others. Anyone else who claims to have this right is either ignorant of the factors involved or, as is more usually the case, an imposter.

As for the doctrinal aspect of Sufi psychology, the human soul is there presented as a substance that possesses different faculties and modes of existence, separated yet united by a single axis that traverses all these modes and planes. There is, moreover, a close link between this psychology and cosmology so that man comes to realize the cosmic dimension of his being, not in a quantitative but in a qualitative and symbolic sense. Moreover, this cosmic correspondence objectivizes the inner structure of the psyche, thereby releasing the soul from its own knots, illuminating its darkest aspects, and displaying to the traveller of the spiritual path the manifold traps lying in his way, in the inner journey of the soul toward its own Centre. The descent to the 'inferno' is the means whereby the soul recovers its lost and hidden elements in dark and lethal depths before being able to make the ascent to 'Purgatory' and 'Paradise'. Sufi psychological doctrine lays this scheme before the adept, in both its microcosmic and macrocosmic aspects, before the actual journey is undertaken. But even this theoretical presentation has the effect of integrating the mental and psychic plane of the person who is able fully to comprehend it.

Eschatology likewise has both a macrocosmic and microcosmic aspect, the latter being what most immediately and directly concerns the adept. From this point of view the posthumous becoming of man is no more than a continuation of the journey on this earth to another level of existence, one which, moreover, can already be undertaken here and now by those who, following the advice of the Prophet, 'موتوا قبل ان تموتوا' 'die before you die', have already died to the life of the carnal soul (*al-nafs al-ammârah*) and been resurrected in the spiritual world. Sufi eschatological doctrines reveal to man the extension of his being beyond the empirical, earthly self with which most human beings identify themselves. These doctrines are therefore again a means whereby the wholeness of the human state in all its amplitude and depth is made known, preparing the ground for the actual realization of the total possibilities of the human condition, a realization which implies the complete integration of man.

The aspects of Sufi doctrine thus delineated address those whose intellectual needs demand such explanation and whose vocation is to think and to know. As for others whose function is to make and to do, in traditional Islamic society Sufism has succeeded in providing means of integration for this group by wedding its symbols to those of the arts and crafts. Through the process of making things the artisan has been able to achieve spiritual perfection and inner integration thanks to the bond created between the guilds (*aṣnâf* and *futuwwât*) and the Sufi orders. The transformations of colour, shape and other accidents that materials undergo in the hands of the artisan came to possess a symbolic significance connected with the transformation of the human soul. And in this same sphere alchemy, which is at once a symbolic science of material forms and a symbolic expression of the spiritual and psychological transformations of the soul, became the link between Sufism and art, and its language the means whereby the maker and the artisan has been given the possibility of integrating his outward and inward life, his work and his religious activity. In this way, as far as the question of the integration of the mind is concerned, the traditional crafts and the methods connected with them came to play a role for the craftsman analogous to that of Sufi doctrine for the contemplative and the thinker.

It may now be asked, what about the contemporary man who is neither metaphysically inclined to understand Sufi doctrine nor practises a traditional craft possessing a spiritual significance and efficacy? Or what about a man who lives in a society where the injunctions of the *Sharî'ah* are not applied and where the mind is therefore likely to be much more dissipated and dispersed? To such questions it must be answered that Sufism possesses the means of integrating man wherever he happens to be, provided man is willing to accept its teachings and discipline. In the cases cited above, methods of meditation are applied which in the absence of a coherent traditional ambience nevertheless enable the final and total integration of man, which includes not only his mind, but his whole being comprising also the body and the psychic and vital forces. Precisely because man is not a dismembered mind but a whole being whereof the mind is an element, doctrine, despite its extreme importance, is not enough: there must also be realization through the practice of a spiritual method. Between the theoretical understanding of the doctrine which integrates the mind and its realization in one's whole being there is a world of difference. In fact without an actual spiritual method too much study of Sufi metaphysics can only cause a further separation between the mind and the rest of one's nature and so make more difficult the final integration of man's total being. That is why doctrine and method are always combined together in all integral traditional spiritual paths like a pair of legs with which man must undertake his spiritual journey.

The role of spiritual method in the integration of man is an essential one, because it is only through the Divine Presence and the *barakah* contained in the methods of Sufism and going back to the origin of the Quranic revelation itself that all of the dispersed elements in man can be brought together. Ordinary man is forever moving away from the centre of his being towards the periphery, dispersing himself in the multiplicity of this world like waves that break up into a thousand drops against the rocks of the sea-shore. This outward-going tendency must be checked and reversed so that man may live inwardly, with his reactions and tendencies moving towards the centre rather than towards the rim; for at the centre resides the One, the Pure and ineffable Being which is the source of all beatitude and goodness, whereas at the periphery is non-existence, which only appears to be real because of man's illusory perception and lack of discrimination. To enter upon the Sufi path, to become initiated into the way or *Ṭarîqah*, is to be given this possibility of reversing the tendency of the soul from the outward to the inward, a change of direction which is possible only through Divine Succour (*tawfîq*) and affirmation (*ta'yîd*) as well as through the *barakah* contained in the methods of Sufism.

In order to bring this transformation about, to turn the attention of the soul from multiplicity to unity, the methods of Sufism base themselves first of all on the practices of the *Sharî'ah*, for Sufism is *Islamic* esotericism and not something else. To practise the *Sharî'ah* is already to gain a measure of integration as a necessary basis as well as by way of foretaste of the complete integration achieved in spiritual realization. Especially the daily prayers are a most powerful means of integrating man's psychic elements and harmonizing them with the corporeal aspect of his being.

The main method of Sufism, in fact, is to extend the prayers so that they become continuous, for as Ḥâfiẓ says: 'خوشا آنان که دائم در نمازند'

'How happy are those who are always praying.'

This extension is not quantitative, but qualitative and vertical; that is, Sufism uses the quintessential form of prayer, the *dhikr* or invocation, in which all otherness and separation from the Divine is removed and man achieves *tawḥîd.* Though this process of transforming man's psyche appears gradual at first, the *dhikr* finishes by becoming man's real nature and the reality with which he identifies himself. With the help of the *dhikr*, as combined with appropriate forms of meditation or *fikr*, man first gains an integrated soul, pure and whole like gold, and then in the *dhikr* he offers this soul to God in the supreme form of sacrifice. Finally in annihilation (*fanâ'*) and subsistence (*baqâ'*) he realizes that he never was separated from God even from the outset.

The integrating power of the *dhikr* is reflected even in the body, whose very structure reflects symbolically man's inner being. Although at the beginning of man's awareness of the spiritual life he must separate himself from the body considered in its negative and passionate aspect, in the more advanced stages of the Path the aim is to keep oneself within the body and centred in the heart, that is, within the body considered in its positive aspect as the 'temple' (*haykal*) of the spirit. The mind is always wandering from one thought to another. To be able to keep it within the body means to be always totally present here and now, in the instant which connects the temporal with the eternal. When Rûmî writes in his *Mathnawî* that the adept must invoke in the spiritual retreat (*khalwah*) until his toes begin to say 'Allâh', he means precisely this final integration which includes the body as well as the mind and the soul. In fact the Islamic and Christian doctrine of corporeal resurrection means above all the complete and total integration of man in the final phase of his becoming.

The man who has achieved integration possesses certain characteristics discernible only by those who are capable of observing them. But the integration of his inner being leaves its effect even upon his outward features, which of necessity reflect his inner states. Such a person is first of all cured of all the maladies of the soul, not by having all tensions and complexes removed in the manner of modern psychoanalysis so that he becomes like a plant quiescent but without an inner drive or attraction toward the Divine, but by having all those tensions which arise from man's profound urge and need for the transcendent realized and fulfilled. Moreover, such a man does not live a compartmentalized existence. His thoughts and actions all issue from a single centre and are based on a series of immutable principles. He has been cured of that hypocrisy in which most men live and therefore, since the veil of otherness which hides the inner light in the majority of men has been removed, like the sun he reflects his light wherever he happens to be. In him, the Islamic ideal of unifying the contemplative and active ways is realized. He does not *either* act *or* think; rather his contemplation and meditation is combined with the purest and most intense activity, And because by virtue of his becoming integrated he reflects Divine Unity and has become the total theophany of the Divine Names and Qualities, he acts and lives in such a manner that there is a spiritual fragrance and beauty about all he does and says. Somehow he is in touch with that *barakah* which runs through the arteries of the Universe.

Islam has always sought to bring about integration and unity, whether it be socially, politically and economically, or morally and intellectually. The integration achieved by Sufism is the essence of this Islamic ideal, realized in such a way that it has always been a supreme example for Islamic society. For the best way to integrate human society is first of all to be integrated oneself. One cannot do good unless one is good, an all too simple truth so often forgotten in the modern world. Nor can one save others unless one has first been saved oneself. Therefore the method of integration contained in Sufism concerns not only the individuals who are affected by it but also casts its light upon the whole of society and is the hidden source for the regeneration of Islamic ethics and the integration of the Islamic community.

The Sufi teaches this simple truth that the basis of all faith or *îmân* is unity, for as Shaykh Maḥmûd Shabistarî writes in his *Gulshan-i-râz*:

یکی بین ویکی گوی ویکی دان　　بدین ختم آمد اصل وفرع ایمان

See but One, say but One, know but One,
In this are summed up the roots and branches of faith.[1]

The integration of man means the realization of the One and the transmutation of the many in the light of the One. It is therefore the full attainment of that faith or *îmân* which is the core and basis of Islam. He who has achieved this inner integration, in sacrificing his soul inwardly to God, also renders the greatest service to Islam and in fact to the truth in whatever form it might be found.

[1] *Mystic Rose Garden,* pp. 84–85.

III

Revelation, Intellect and Reason in the Quran

One of the most unfortunate tendencies prevalent in certain quarters in the Islamic world today is to adopt an ideology that happens to be fashionable in the Western world and then attach the adjective 'Islamic' to it. Thus we see such terms as 'Islamic Democracy' or 'Islamic Socialism' or 'Islamic Rationalism' or the like. This tendency, in attempting to make Islam acceptable by making it appear modern or up-to-date, betrays Islam by reducing it from a total body of principles and from a complete world-view to an adjective modifying a noun, which has a completely different connotation in the matrix of the Western civilization that has given birth to these terms.

In fact, Islam can only gain respect and even adherence among intelligent non-Muslims as well as young, Western-educated Muslims themselves by being expounded, not as another version of such Western ideologies as happen to be fashionable today, but as a clear-cut alternative to these ideologies presenting a complete programme for life itself and for man's whole endeavour in this world.

If the defence of Islam is to be based on a set of weak, ever-retreating apologetics whose technique is to make everything fashionable appear as Islamic, it can hardly convince the thoughtful. Moreover, such methods will make Islam appear to the intelligent observer as a second-rate Western ideology. If Islam is presented, for example, as socialism or rationalism, then the thoughtful modern man who stands outside the world of faith will seek the purer form of socialism and rationalism in the Western philosophies and ideologies themselves, rather than in their Islamic imitation.

There are certain modern Muslims who in the name of what they believe to be a simple rationalistic Islam, which they feel will accord with the modern world, are willing to brush aside fourteen centuries of Islamic civilization and intellectual heritage together with the schools of wisdom and philosophy cultivated therein. Little are they aware of the fact that the major problems posed by the modern world for religion, whether these challenges be Marxism or Darwinism or secular existentialism, can be answered, not by a simple rationalistic interpretation of Islam in the manner of the Ṣalafiyyah school and its like, but by appealing to that profound metaphysical and philosophical treasury of wisdom of a traditional character cultivated in Islam and connected for the most part with Sufism, a wisdom which while being logical and rational is not simply rationalistic.

This brings up the question as to what rationalism means exactly in the Western languages. One must distinguish between the normal use of reason and logic, and rationalism, which makes of reason the sole instrument for gaining knowledge and the only criterion for judging the truth. One does sometimes speak of Aristotelian rationalism, although in the philosophy of Aristotle there are metaphysical intuitions which cannot be reduced to simple products of the human reason; but rationalism in the proper sense of the word begins in modern European philosophy, although there are also cases of it in late Antiquity.

If by Rationalism one means an attempt to build a closed system embracing the whole of reality and based upon human reason alone, then this begins with Descartes, since for him the ultimate criterion of reality itself is the human ego and not the Divine Intellect or Pure Being. His *cogito ergo sum* places a limitation upon human knowledge by binding it to the level of individual reason and to the consciousness of the individual ego. It is this tendency which reaches its culmination with eighteenth- and nineteenth-century rationalism, before the very heaviness of the rationalistic system begins to produce cracks in its own protective wall, through which irrational elements begin to flow in from below.

In seeking to understand the role of reason in Islam it is essential to distinguish between rationalism as described above and respect for logic, because on its own level logic is an aspect of the truth and truth (*al-ḥaqq*) is a name of Allah. Intelligence is likewise a divine gift which leads man to an affirmation of the doctrine of unity (*al-tawḥîd*) and of the essential verities of the Islamic revelation. The use of logic in the world view of Islam is like that of a ladder which leads man from the world of multiplicity up towards the Divine.

Rationalism as it developed in the West—a West in which the traditional Christian man was bound to God more by his will than by his intelligence, as is the case in Islam—became a veil which separated man from God and marked the human revolt against heaven.

The result of the application of logic and intelligence in Islam is the mosque whose symmetry and regularity is an occasion for the contemplation of the Divine Presence. The result of the application of modern Western science, which is embedded in seventeenth-century rationalism, is the modern factory or skyscraper which like the mosque is geometrical and sometimes symmetrical, but which is marked particularly by its lack of a transcendent connotation and in fact represents the works of that type of man who has rebelled against God. In the difference between these two applications of logic, between the traditional Muslim mosque or house and the modern skyscraper or apartment building, one can see the profound difference between rationalism in the West and the use of reason and logic in Islam.

As a matter of fact one of the great services that Islam can render to the modern world, in which the dichotomy between reason and revelation or science and religion has reached such dangerous proportions, is to represent this possibility of the union between revelation and reason as found in the Quran. The source of revelation in Islam is the Archangel Gabriel or the Universal Intellect. Intellect (*al-'aql al-kullî* in the language of *ḥadîth*) and the word *'aql* itself signify etymologically both that which binds or limits the Absolute in the direction of creation and also that which binds man to the truth, to God himself. In the perspective of Islam it is precisely *'aql* which keeps man on the straight path (the *ṣirâṭ al-mustaqîm*) and prevents him from going astray. That is why so many verses of the Quran equate those who go astray with those who cannot use their intellect (as in the verses *wa lā ya'qilūn*, 'they do not understand' or literally 'use their intellect'—the verb *ya'qilūn* deriving from the root *'aqala* which is related to *'aql*; or the verse *lā yafqahūn*, 'they understand not', the verb *yafqahūn* being related to the root *faqiha* which again means comprehension or knowledge.)

Likewise knowledge or science (*al-'ilm*) in the language of the Quran and the *Ḥadīth* means that knowledge which makes man aware of God, of the eternal verities, of the world to come and the return to God. This is an undeniable truth even though so many modern Muslim apologists equate *'ilm* without even a restriction or modification with modern science as if one could overcome the profound difference in the types of knowledge involved by simply using the same term to connote the diverse types of science in question. Some *ḥadîths* have simply equated *'ilm* with knowledge of the other world, *al-âkhirah*. The Intellect, the instrument through which this type of knowledge is obtained, which is at once the source of revelation and exists microcosmically within man, must not be mistaken for reason alone. The *'aql* is at once both *intellectus* or *nous* and *ratio* or reason. It is both the supernal sun that shines within man and the reflection of this sun on the plane of the mind which we call reason.

One can go from the reflection to the source provided the *'aql* is not dimmed by passions, provided it is the wholesome, balanced and harmonious Intellect which in Islamic terminology is called *al-'aql al-salîm*. But if the *'aql* is obscured by the passions, by the *nafs*, then it can become the veil that hides man from the Divine and leads him astray. Were this not to be so, there would be no need for revelation at all. Revelation is the macrocosmic manifestation of the Universal Intellect, the *Kalimat Allâh*, which provides a framework for the microcosmic manifestation of the Intellect in man and a Divine Law which protects man from his own passions and makes it possible for the intellect to remain wholesome or *salîm*.

Reason, this reflection of the Intellect upon the level of the psyche, can then be both an instrument for reaching the divine truths found in revelation, truths which are super-rational but not irrational, and a veil which hides these very truths from man. In the latter case it becomes the means whereby man rebels against God and His revealed religion.

Muslim sages throughout the ages have recognized this two-edged nature of the sword of reason. Some like Ghazzâlî, Jalâl al-Dîn Rûmî and Fakhr al-Dîn Râzî have emphasized the negative aspect of purely human reason as veil and limitation and its inability to reach the divine verities. Rûmî in fact was very conscious of the difference between reason (*'aql-i juz'î*) and intellect (*'aql-i kullî*) when he said 'It is reason which has destroyed the reputation of the Intellect.' (عقل جزئی عقل را بدنام کرد).

Others like Ibn Sînâ, Ibn 'Arabî and Ṣadr al-Dîn Shîrâzî have sought to reach the Intellect through reason itself, to make use of logic and the rational faculties of man to lead man above and beyond these faculties and planes.

It would be sheer folly to ignore these two aspects of reason by equating Islam with rationalism instead of benefiting from the immense treasury of Islamic wisdom wherein this problem is elaborated, especially in the treatises of Sufism. What logical grounds has one to hope that somehow the results of rationalism in Islam will be different from what happened in Christian Europe? If Islam is to avoid the fatal dichotomy between faith and reason and counteract the already existing tendency of some of the younger generation to become alienated from Islam as a result of their first contact with Western science and philosophy, it must preserve and make known to all concerned the hierarchy of knowledge that has always been an essential feature of the Islamic world-view.

One cannot harmonize the Quran and science simply by equating such and such a verse of the Quran with a particular scientific discovery which moreover soon will become outmoded. The Quran does not provide a detailed science of things but the principles of all knowledge. What can be done is to preserve and revivify a total world view, a metaphysics having its roots in the Quran and deriving from the light of the Intellect, a light which is so intimately bound with the Quran as regards both its source and its content. In the light of this wisdom one can then bring into being a philosophy of both nature and man such as will do full justice to the needs of reason, without falling into the trap of an agnostic and Promethean rationalism.

The whole world, both Muslim and non-Muslim, is in need of this wisdom and the philosophy of man based upon it. Moreover, this wisdom can only be resuscitated and brought once again to life in terms of modern modes of expression by turning to the immensely rich intellectual heritage of Islam, not by destroying this heritage and turning to a flat rationalism devoid of any transcendent dimension. In providing a solution based on the hierarchy of knowledge and on the harmony between faith and reason deriving from the Intellect, which is the source of both faith and reason, Islam can offer a message of utmost significance to the whole world. Instead of picking up the bread-crumbs of the table of Western thinkers and trying to add the label Islamic to them, Islam can provide its own fresh vision of the relation between reason and revelation or science and religion—as well as that between man and nature, wherein lies the root of the present ecological crisis. This vision is of vital importance for the future of Islam, and also one which many thoughtful people throughout the world are seeking desperately. May the intellectual leaders of the Islamic world succeed in carrying out this task of providing a fresh vision of the traditional teachings of Islam; there can be no more vital task than this.

IV

The Sufi Master as Exemplified in Persian Sufi Literature

No authentic spiritual path is possible without a master and Sufism is certainly no exception to this universal principle. The Sufi master is the representative of the esoteric function of the Prophet of Islam and by the same token he is the theophany of Divine Mercy which lends itself to those willing to turn to it. The *Sharî'ah*, the Divine Law, is meant for all Muslims, and in fact from the Islamic point of view, for all men, if its universal meaning be considered. But the *Ṭarîqah*, or spiritual path, is meant only for those who seek God here and now and who search after that immutable Truth which, although present here and now, is at the same time the transcendent and eternal source of all revelation. The *Ṭarîqah* is thus a means whereby man can return to the origin of the Islamic revelation itself and become in a spiritual sense both a companion and successor of the Prophet and the saints.

The role of the spiritual master, the *shaykh*, *murshid*, *murâd*, or *pîr*, as he is known in Arabic, Persian and other Muslim languages, is to make this spiritual rebirth and transformation possible. Being himself connected through the chain of initiation (*silsilah*) to the Prophet and to the function of initiation (*walâyah*)[1] inherent in the prophetic mission itself, the Sufi master is able to deliver man from the narrow confines of the material world into the illimitable luminous space of the spiritual life. Through him, acting as the representative of the Prophet, spiritual death and rebirth take place by virtue of the *barakah* which he carries within himself.

Fallen man grows old, decays and dies, whereas the regenerated spiritual man is always inwardly in the prime of youth. Having drunk from the fountain of eternal life and having gained access to the elixir of immortality he lives in the perennial spring of the soul even if his body passes through the winter of life. And that is why the master is able to endow the disciple with youth, whatever may be his chrono-

[1] The term *walî* in the context of Sufism means 'saint'. The Arabic root besides meaning 'friend' also possesses the meaning of dominion or power. From this root the terms *wilâyah* and *walâyah* are formed, the first meaning sanctity and the second the initiatic power or function as such. In Shi'ism especially, the distinction between 'the cycle of prophecy' (*dâ'irat al-nubuwwah*) and 'the cycle of initiation' (*dâ'irat al-walâyah*) is emphasized, as we shall discuss later in chapter VIII.

logical age. To behold the perfect master is to regain the ecstasy and joy of the spring of life and to be separated from the master is to experience the sorrow of old age.

> I aged with his affliction, but when Tabrîz
> You name, all my youth comes back to me.[2]

Man may seek the fountain of life by himself. He may seek to discover the principles of spiritual regeneration through his own efforts. But this endeavour is in vain and will never bear fruit unless the master is present together with the discipline which only he can impart. Without the philosopher's stone no alchemical transformation is possible. Only the power of the *shaykh* can deliver man from himself—from his carnal soul—so as to enable him to behold the Universe as it really is and to rejoin the sea of Universal Existence.

> Without the power imperial of Shamsu'l-Ḥaqq of Tabrîz
> One could neither behold the moon nor become the sea.[3]

To be sure, there are those rare people such as the Uwaysîs who are initiated into the way by Khaḍir or Khiḍr, the prophet possessing an unusually long life who can initiate men into the Divine Mysteries and who corresponds in many ways to Enoch in the Judaeo-Christian tradition, or by the 'men of the invisible hierarchy' (*rijâl al-ghayb*), or, in the case of Shi'ism, by the Hidden Imâm who is the spiritual pole (*Quṭb*) of the Universe. But these exceptional ways, which are in any case not for men to choose and to seek but for which a few are chosen, nevertheless pertain to the universal initiatic function of which the Sufi master is the embodiment on earth. Inwardly united with the invisible hierarchy and the Truth (*al-ḥaqq*) itself, he appears outwardly among men as the sign of the supreme mercy (*raḥmah*) of God, as the means whereby man can gain access to the spiritual world and be admitted to the company of prophets and saints. He is the door through which one must pass in order to enter

[2] R. A. Nicholson, *Selected Poems from the Dîvâni Shamsi Tabrîz*, Cambridge, 1952, p. 25. Shams-i Tabrîzî was the spiritual master of the greatest Sufi poet of the Persian language, Jalâl al-Dîn Rûmî, and also for him the perfect theophany of the Divine Names and Qualities, the total exemplar of the Universal Man. The *Dîwân* especially, contains some of the most beautiful and profound verses in Persian on the function of the spiritual master and the relation between master and disciple. The name of Shams-i Tabrîzî (Shams al-Dîn meaning the 'sun of religion') is itself highly symbolic and Rûmî often uses the symbolism of the name in verses which seem to refer both to the master and to the Divine Truth Itself, alluding again and again to the inner union of the master with God.

[3] Nicholson, *op. cit.* p. 79.

'the garden of the Beloved' while at the same time he is the guide to the inner court of this garden.

To become initiated into a Sufi order and to accept the discipleship of a master is to enter into a bond that is permanent, surviving even death. For the disciple the *shaykh* is always mysteriously present, especially during the rituals. The *shaykh* never dies for the disciple even if he has physically left this world. His spiritual guidance (*irshâd*) and assistance continue even after death. The spiritual master, whom Rûmî calls the heavenly rider, comes and goes, but the dust of his galloping remains. His effect upon his disciples is permanent and the seed he has sown in their hearts continues to be nurtured and cared for, even after the temple of his body has fallen into dust. Under his care, even from this earthly ruin the seed can grow into a tree which stretches to heaven and extends from the Eastern to the Western horizons.[4]

Slave, be aware
The lord of all the East[5] is here;
The glittering storm-cloud of eternity
Reveals his lightning-flash to thee.
Whate'ver thou sayest
Is but as inference has guessed;
He speaks upon the eye's experience,
And therein lies the difference.
The heavenly rider passed;
The dust rose in the air;
He sped; but the dust he cast
Yet hangeth there.
Straight forward thy vision be,
And gaze not left or right,
His dust is here, and he
In the Infinite.[6]

[4] It must, of course, be remembered that initiation into Sufism by a master does not in itself guarantee realization. The disciple must be firm in his devotion to the master and in performing his religious and initiatic duties. He must love God more than the world and be attached to Him not only through a theoretical comprehension of Sufi metaphysics but also by a total 'ontological' attachment. The Divine succour and aid (*tawfîq*) must also be present, without which nothing is possible. The gardener sows many seeds in the ground: not all of them grow to be plants that will bear fruit.

[5] Since the name Shams al-Dîn means the 'sun of religion' and the sun rises in the East, Rûmî often employs the universal symbolism of East and West as realms of light and darkness and refers to his master as the 'lord of the East' again implying his union with the source of all light.

[6] A. J. Arberry, *The Rubâ'îyât of Jalâl al-Dîn Rûmî*, London, 1949, p. 19.

Likewise the assembly (*majlis*) of the Sufi master is a terrestrial image of the heavenly assembly of the saints. The disciple (*faqîr*) who gains the right of entry into this assembly by virtue of having been initiated by the master also gains for himself a place in the assembly of paradise, provided he remains faithful to the master and his instructions. Once he fulfils the conditions of discipleship and reaches perfection in the assembly, his station becomes of permanent importance and gains a significance beyond the life of this world and beyond the grave. The master leaves a permanent mark upon the disciple by virtue of which the disciple who has reached perfection again joins the assembly of his master in the other world. By the perfection gained in the *majlis* of the Sufis, the *faqîr* gains access to the royal assembly of heaven and constructs for himself an exalted abode in the afterlife.

And, O friend, if you reach perfection in our assembly (*majlis*)
Your seat will be the throne, you will gain your desire in all things.
But if you stay many years more in this earth,
You will pass from place to place, you will be as the dice in backgammon.
If Shamsi Tabrîz draws you to his side,
When you escape from captivity you will return to that orb.[7]

Not only is the influence of the *shaykh* permanent but also his light is everywhere. Though distinct as a spiritual personality, he is inwardly identified with the light that shines upon the land and sea and illuminates all things for the disciple who is closely attached to him.

From Tabrîz-ward shone the Sun of Truth, and I said to him:
'Thy light is at once joined with all things and apart from all.'[8]

It is this light that shines upon the heart of the disciple and converts it from something corruptible and perishable to an incorruptible and eternal substance. It is the spiritual influence of the *shaykh* that transforms the transient and passing into the abiding and everlasting.

The sun of the face of Shamsi Dîn, glory of the horizons,
Never shone upon aught perishable but he made it eternal.[9]

Not everyone who claims to be a Sufi master possesses all the qualifications that make for the perfect master. Not only must the

[7] Nicholson, *op. cit.*, p. 187.
[8] *Ibid.*, p. 27.
[9] *Ibid.*, p. 111.

disciple seek a master, but he must also be sure that the *shaykh* or ***pîr*** to whom he is surrendering himself is a seasoned guide who can lead through the dangerous precipices of the Way to the final goal of realization. Otherwise there is a danger of deviation through the corruption of what is most precious in man. With an incompetent guide, it is best not to climb mountains but to remain on flat ground where a fall is less likely to be fatal.

The *shaykh* must have a clear and regular connection with the chain of initiation and a realization of the truths of the Path. Moreover, he must be chosen from on high to fulfil the function of guiding others. Even among those who have advanced on the Way, not everyone is qualified to become a master. The master is chosen by the hand of Divine Mercy to guide men. He cannot claim to fulfil this function simply by his own will. If he is to be an effective master he must know the details and intricacies of the Path and also the soul and psychic substance of the disciple whom he is to guide. Not only is the presence of a perfect *shaykh* necessary but he must also be a master who has the qualifications for guiding a particular disciple. Not every *shaykh* is a master for every disciple. The disciple must seek and find the master who conquers his soul and dominates him as an eagle or falcon pounces upon a sparrow in the air.

> O Splendour of the Truth, Ḥusâmu'ddîn,[10] take one or two sheets of paper and add (them to the poem) in description of the Pîr.
> Although thy slender body hath no strength, yet without the sun (of thy spirit) we have no light.
> Although thou hast become the lighted wick and the glass (lamp), yet thou art the heart's leader (the Spiritual Guide): thou art the end of the thread (which serves as a clue).
> Inasmuch as the end of the thread is in thy hand and will, the beads (of spiritual knowledge) on the heart's necklace are (derived) from thy bounty.
> Write down what appertains to the Pîr (Guide) who knows the Way: choose the Pîr and regard him as the essence of the Way.
> The Pîr is (like) summer, and (other) people are (like) the autumn month; (other) people are like night, and the Pîr is the moon.
> I have bestowed on (my) young Fortune (Ḥusâmu'ddîn) the name of Pîr (old), because he is (made) old by the Truth, not (made) old by Time.

[10] When writing the *Mathnawî*, Rûmî's spiritual pole of attraction was Ḥusâm al-Dîn, the figure who is so often cited in the *Mathnawî*.

So old is he that he hath no beginning: there is no rival to such a unique Pearl.
Verily, old wine grows more potent; verily, old gold is more highly prized.
Choose a Pîr, for without a Pîr this journey is exceeding full of woe and affright and danger.
Without an escort you are bewildered (even) on a road you have travelled many times (before):
Do not, then, travel alone on a Way that you have not seen at all, do not turn your head away from the Guide.[11]

To accept initiatic guidance from one who is not a perfect master is most dangerous, for it may completely spoil the possibility of spiritual realization and even open the soul to demonic influences. The potentiality of growth is present within men, but if it is not actualized correctly, it will become spoiled and like a spoilt seed never be able to grow into a tree.

'As for the master (*murâd*), in the sense of one who is initiated and followed, he is one whose initiatic power (*walâyah*) in influencing others has reached the degree of perfecting those who are imperfect and who has seen (initiatically) the different kinds of capabilities and ways of guiding and training disciples. Such a person is either a traveller attracted by Divine Grace (*sâlik-i majdhûb*), who has first traversed all the deserts and precipices of the carnal soul through travelling upon the Path (*sulûk*), and then with the help of Divine attraction has returned from the stations of the heart and ascensions of the spirit, and has reached the world of vision and certainty and joined the state of contemplation and examination. Or he is one attracted by Divine Grace who travels on the Path (*majdhûb-i sâlik*), who first through the help of Divine attraction has traversed the extent of the stations and has reached the world of vision and unveiling of the Divine realities and then has crossed again the stations and stages of the Path through travelling (*sulûk*) and has rediscovered the truth of contemplation in the form of knowledge.

'The degree of being a spiritual guide worthy of imitation is certain in the case of these two types of men. As for the unripe traveller (*sâlik*), who has not as yet left the narrow strait of spiritual struggle and endeavour to reach the space of spiritual vision, or the unripe person attracted by Divine Grace (*majdhûb*), who has not as yet become aware of the intricacies of travelling upon the Path or of the realities of the stations and stages and of the pitfalls and dangerous

[11] Rûmî, *Mathnawî*, trans. R. A. Nicholson, vol. II, London, 1926, pp. 160–1.

passages of the Way, neither of these two has as yet the right to the station and rank of spiritual master (*shaykhûkhat*); the initiatic power of influencing the spiritual capabilities of the adept and training the disciples according to the laws of the Path (*ṭarîqah*) has not been entrusted to them. Whatever conquest they make in the souls of men in this sense is more harmful than beneficial.

'The existence of the disciple and the potentiality of spiritual perfection in him can be likened to an egg in which there exists the potentiality of becoming a bird. If the egg has the capability of receiving the power and influence inherent in the spiritual will (*himmat*) of the bird or the master, if it can gain the protection of a mature bird in whom the power of procreation and the causing of the egg to hatch has become actualized, and finally if for a period the influence of the spiritual life and the characteristics which belong to the state of birdhood affect the egg, then at last it will cease to remain in the form of an egg. It will be dressed in the form of a bird and made to reach the perfection of its capabilities. And if the egg is placed under a hen who does not possess the power of flight or has not as yet reached the degree of maturity and power to make the egg hatch, and this goes on for some time, the potentiality of becoming a bird is destroyed in it and then there will be no way of restoring the egg to its original state.

'Likewise, if the sincere disciple places himself in complete obedience and submission under the control of a perfect master who has attained the degree of perfection and in whom travelling upon the Path, flight, spiritual march and attraction to the Divine Grace are combined, from the egg of his existence the bird of the truth "Verily God created Adam in His image" will come forth, a bird which will then fly in the space of spiritual identity and reach the degree of procreation and generation. But if he comes under the influence of an unripe traveller (*sâlik*) or an unripe person attracted by Divine Grace (*majdhûb*), then the possibility of the perfection of the human state will become spoiled in him. He will not reach the excellence of spiritual men (*rijâl*) or the station of perfection.'[12]

The disciple must surrender himself to the perfect *shaykh* without any reserve. In the hands of the master he must be like a corpse in the hands of the washer of the dead without any movement of its own. The master is the representative of the Prophet and through him of God. To take his hand is to accept the 'Hand of the Divine'.

> God has declared that his (the Pîr's) hand is as His own, since He
> gave out (the words) *the Hand of God is above their hands.*

[12] 'Izz al-Dîn Kâshânî, *Miṣbâḥ al-hidâyah*, ed. J. Humâ'î, Tehran, 1323 (A. H. Solar), pp. 108–9 (translated from the Persian by S. H. Nasr).

The Hand of God causes him (the child) to die and (then) brings him to life. What of life? He makes him a spirit everlasting.[13]

The role of the Sufi master to whom one must make perfect surrender and his significance in delivering the disciple from bewilderment in the world of multiplicity and leading him to contemplation in the world of Unity are well exemplified in the spiritual testament of Shams al-'Urafâ' ('the sun of the gnostics'), one of the leading Sufi masters of the present century in Persia. Shams al-'Urafâ' described his meeting with his master and the subsequent transformations that overcame him as follows:

'This humble *faqîr*, Sayyid Ḥusayn ibn al-Riḍâ al-Ḥusaynî al-Ṭihrânî al-Ni'matullâhî, was blessed with divine favour in the year 1303 (A.H.) when I met his gracious Holiness, the model of gnostics and the pole of orientation of the travellers upon the Path, the honourable direction of prayers, Shaykh 'Abd al-Quddûs Kirmân-shâhî. At this time all my attention was directed to the study of the formal (traditional) sciences and I possessed some knowledge of medicine, philosophy, mathematics, geometry, astronomy and astrology, jurisprudence and its principles, grammar, geography and prosody and was occupied with studying and teaching. But I had no knowledge of the problems of Sufism and the laws of spiritual poverty and gnosis and was unaware of the science of the truth and the intricacies of Divine knowledge. My attention was turned only to the problems of the formal sciences and the debates and discussions of text-books but not to inner purification, embellishment and contemplation. I had made no endeavour on the path of purifying the soul and cleansing the inner being, thinking that the way to know the truth is none other than pursuing the formal sciences.

'Thanks to Divine Grace and the aid of the Pure Imâms—upon whom be peace—I met that great man on the above-mentioned date near Imâm-Zâdih Zayd.[14] He did with me what he did. Again within the distance of a week I was blessed with his presence near Imâm-Zâdih Zayd.

'After some conversation I expressed the wish to become initiated. On Thursday night I went to the bath at his side and received the ritual ablutions that he had ordered. After the bath he took my hand in the customary fashion and after performing the formula of repentance he instructed and initiated me to the invocation (*dhikr*) of the heart with the litanies (*awrâd*), the particular initiating acts and

[13] *Mathnawî*, vol. II, p. 162.
[14] A tomb of a saint near Tehran.

invocations. I obeyed. After fifteen nights [the minor retreat (*khalwat-i ṣaghîr*)] near the hour of dawn, while in contemplation, I saw all the doors and walls of the dark room in which I was placed participating in the invocation with me.

'I fainted and fell. After sunrise my corporeal father, because of the great love he had for me, did not stop at any measure in bringing a physician and calling those who attract the *jinn* (psychic forces) or write prayers to cure illness. My corporeal mother also did all possible in the way of administering different medicines, inhalents and nourishments.

'For twenty days I was in such a condition. I could not perform the duties laid down by the *Sharî'ah* nor was I aware of formal customs. I spoke to no one concerning this matter. After this period my condition returned somewhat to normal and I became free from the state of "attraction" (*jadhbah*). I went to the bath and purified myself. I felt the desire to meet that great master and for a few days I wandered like a madman in the streets and bazaars seeking him. Finally I succeeded in meeting him. I kissed his hand and he expressed his benevolence towards me.

'To summarize: for two years I travelled upon the spiritual Path under his care and following his instructions. I turned away completely from the formal sciences and endeavoured to understand questions of gnosis and to march upon the Path of certainty. Whatever he ordered I obeyed without saying yes or no. If some of the things I heard or saw appeared on the surface to be opposed to the *Sharî'ah*, I considered it a defect of my own ears and eyes and did not fail in any way to serve and obey him. In service, conversation, solitude and retreat I obeyed as completely as I could. I also obeyed all that he had ordered as necessary in the six kinds of invocation: the manifested (*jaliy*), the hidden (*khafiy*), the informal (*ḥamâ'ilî*), the obscure (*khumûlî*), that connected with the circle (*ḥalqah*) and with the gathering (*ijtimâ'*). I was also made to realize the four houses of death. . . .

'Thanks be to God, through the spiritual will of my master and the assistance of the saints I realized all the seven states of the heart and fulfilled in the way of actions and litanies whatever was required for each station. I performed the minor, middle and major "forty days" (*arba'înât*) [of spiritual retreat]. In the year 1309 (A.H.) I accompanied him to the city of faith, Qum, and there performed two consecutive major "forty days". His Holiness joined the Divine Mercy (died) there and I became very ill without my intimate friend and comforter. I passed days and nights in hardship at the corner of the mosque of Imâm Ḥasan until my poor mother discovered my condition and sent someone to Qum who for a while treated me. After some improvement I returned to Tehran with that friend.

'Thank God through the spiritual will of that great gnostic I came to know of the details of spiritual poverty, gnosis, the subtleties of realized knowledge and certainty, and reached the station of annihilation in God (*fanâ'*) and subsistence in Him (*baqâ'*). I travelled the seven stations of the heart each with its special characteristics. With his esoteric aid and assistance from the intermediate world (*barzakh*), whatever order I received concerning commands or prohibitions, cleanliness, worship, asceticism, spiritual retreat, or self-purification I performed fully and did not fall short of serving God's creatures as far as I could.'[15]

In speaking of the Sufi master in the Persian context one must remember the role of the Twelfth Imâm, who is the Hidden Imâm, both in Shi'ism and in Sufism as it exists in the Shi'ite world. Inasmuch as the Imâm, although in concealment, is alive and is the spiritual axis of the world, he is the pole (*Quṭb*) with whom all Sufi masters are inwardly connected. He is to Shi'ism what the supreme pole is to Sufism in its Sunni context. In Shi'ism the Imâms, especially 'Alî, the first, and the Mahdî, the last, are the spiritual guides *par excellence*. The Hidden Imâm, representing the whole chain of Imâms, is the pole that attracts the hearts of the believers and it is to him that men turn for guidance.

Moreover, the Imâm also exists within the hearts of men. He is the inner guide who can lead man on the journey beyond the cosmos and also into the inner dimensions of his own being, if only man could reach this inner pole. That is why certain Shi'ite gnostics and Sufis have instructed the disciple to seek the '*imâm* of his being'. The possessor of the power of *walâyah* or initiation, by virtue of which the Imâm in fact becomes the Imâm, is the esoteric interpreter of things, of religion and of nature. And it is, in the Shi'ite view, the Imâm's inward connection with the Sufi masters that enables them to gain the power of initiating and guiding men so that these men too can in fact reach the inner pole of their being.

It can therefore be said that despite a difference of view in Shi'ite and Sunni Islam as to the identity of the *Quṭb*, which Sunnism does not identify distinctly but Shi'ism considers to be the Hidden Imâm or the function of the Imâm as such, both agree as to the presence of this universal initiatic function (*walâyah*) which exists within Islam as

[15] 'Abd al-Ḥujjat Balâghî, *Maqâlât al-ḥunafâ' fî maqâmât Shams al-'Urafâ'*, Tehran, 1327 (A. H. Solar), pp. 232–4 (translated from the Persian by S. H. Nasr).

within every integral tradition. The Sufi masters are those unique individuals who through their connection with this golden chain of initiation are called upon by God to keep the presence of the spiritual Way alive on this earth and to guide upon this royal Path those who possess the necessary qualifications. They are thus the princes of the spiritual world. In their hands the desert blooms into a garden, base metal is turned into gold and the chaotic state of the soul is crystallized into a pattern of beauty reflecting the perfume of Unity (*al-tawḥîd*).

> Make a journey out of self into self, O master,
> For by such a journey earth becomes a quarry of gold.
> From sourness and bitterness advance to sweetness,
> Even as from briny soil a thousand sorts of fruits spring up.
> From the sun, the pride of Tabrîz, behold these miracles,
> For every tree gains beauty by the light of the sun.[16]

[16] Nicholson, *op. cit.*, p. 111.

V

The Spiritual States in Sufism

A major portion of Sufi treatises throughout the ages has dealt with the spiritual states[1] which the adept experiences and passes through in his journey upon the Way (*ṭarīqah*) to God. The insistence of Sufi masters upon this theme either in the form of the enumeration of the stations and states of the Path or the listing of the spiritual virtues which must be gained by the disciple is due to the fundamental significance of the knowledge of spiritual states for anyone who aspires to pass through them and beyond them to the Divine Presence. If we put aside the erroneous and truncated concept of man as a creature formed only of body and mind, a concept that is due more than anything else to Cartesian dualism along with a misunderstanding of certain tenets of scholasticism, and return to the traditional conception of man as being comprised of body, soul and Spirit (the *corpus*, *anima* and *spiritus* of Hermeticism and other sapiential doctrines) the relevance of the spiritual states becomes more clear. The Spirit is like the sky, shining and immutable above the horizons of the soul. It is a world which, although not yet God, is inseparable from Him so that to reach it is already to be in the front courtyard of paradise and the proximity of the Divine. The body also bears in its objective and natural existence, although not necessarily in its subjective prolongation in the psyche, the 'vestiges of the Creator' (*vestigio Dei*) so that it can be considered as the temple of the Spirit and can play a completely positive role in the very process of spiritual realization.[2]

What remains of man, namely the soul or *anima*, is precisely the subject of the spiritual work. This is the lead that must be transmuted into gold, the moon that must become wed to the Sun, and at the same time the dragon that must be slain in order that the hero may reach the treasure. Man in his unregenerated and 'fallen' state, to

[1] For the moment one is using the term 'state' in its general sense, whereas according to technical Sufi terminology there is a difference between state (*ḥāl*) and station (*maqām*), to which we shall turn later in this chapter.

[2] The body considered as the temple of the Spirit is found in Hesychasm in Christianity as well as in many forms of Hinduism and Buddhism. Suhrawardī uses 'Temples of Light' (*Hayākil al-nūr*) as the title of one of his most famous works drawing on the same symbolism.

use the Christian terminology, is the subject addressed by treatises on spiritual discipline. A man in such a state is precisely one who identifies himself solely with his psychic substance or mind, not realizing that this is but the reflection of the Intellect on the psychic plane. He identifies himself with the soul that has not as yet experienced the liberating contact with the Spirit and he lives imprisoned in a world of sense impressions deriving from the body, along with the logical inferences drawn from that world, and in an unilluminated subjective labyrinth that is filled with passionate impulses. The spiritual path is none other than the process of disentangling the roots of the soul from the psycho-physical world to which they are attached and plunging them in the Divine. It means therefore a radical transformation of the soul, made possible through the grace of revelation and initiation, until the soul becomes worthy of becoming the bride of the Spirit and entering into union with it. To reach God, the soul must become God-like. Hence the significance of the spiritual stations and states that the soul must experience and the spiritual virtues which it must acquire and which mark the degrees of the ascent of the soul toward God. In fact each virtue *is* a station through which the soul must pass and which it must experience in a permanent way.

If we recall the well-known definition of Sufism by Junayd—'Sufism is that God makes thee die to thyself and become resurrected in Him'[3]—we shall understand that the gaining of the spiritual virtues and their corresponding states and stations are so many stages in the death of the soul in respect of its base and accidental nature, and its resurrection *in divinis*. That is why the highest of the virtues is truthfulness, which stands opposed to all the dark tendencies of the soul, and the highest of stations is subsistence in God, which is none other than resurrection in Him. The end of Sufism is of course to reach God, the Truth (*al-ḥaqq*), and not to acquire a particular station. But since man is not just an intelligence that can discern the Truth and know the Absolute but also a will, the virtues are a necessary concomitant to the total attachment of man to the Truth. For, 'Truth, when it appears on the level of the will, becomes virtue, and it is then veracity and sincerity.'[4] Likewise, because the end of Sufism is God and not the world of action nor any creaturely gain, the virtues are not just moral acts but inner states that are never

[3] Farīd al-Dīn 'Aṭṭār, *Tadhkirat al-awliyā'*, ed. by R. A. Nicholson, Leiden, 1322, Part II, pp. 35–6.

[4] F. Schuon, *Spiritual Perspectives and Human Facts*, trans. by D. M. Matheson, London, 1953, p. 172.

separated from the intellectual and spiritual significance attaching to the world of the Spirit. 'Truths make us understand the virtues and give them all their cosmic fullness and their spiritual efficacy. As for the virtues, they lead us into truths and transform them for us into realities that are concrete, seen and lived.'[5]

If the discussion of spiritual states in Sufism is inseparable from that of the virtues (*maḥāsin* or *faḍā'il*), it is precisely because in Sufism a virtue is seen not as an act or external attribute but as a manner of being. It has a definite ontological aspect. That is why in the classical enumeration of the states and stations of the soul we always meet with the enumeration of the virtues. A state or station, like patience (*ṣabr*) or confidence (*tawakkul*), *is* a virtue, which means that when the soul reaches such a state not only does it possess the virtue in question as an accident, but its very substance is transformed by it so that during that stage of the Way in a sense it *is* itself that virtue. It is this ontological dimension of the virtues that makes the discussion of them inseparable from that of the spiritual states, as we see in so many Sufi treatises, old and new. Of course the Sufis never tire of emphasizing that the end of Sufism is not to possess such and such a virtue or state as such but to reach God beyond all states and virtues. But to reach the Transcendent beyond the virtues, man must first possess the virtues; to reach the station of annihilation and subsistence in God, man must have already passed through the other states and stations.

'The Sufis,' says Abu'l-Ḥasan al-Nūrī, one of the disciples of Junayd, 'are those people whose souls have become cleansed of the impurity of human nature [in its purely creaturely aspect]. They are those who have become pure from the wretchedness of the carnal soul and free from desire until they have come to rest in the forefront and in the highest degree with God. They fled from all that is other than He. They possess nothing and are possessed by nothing.'[6] It is this cleansing of the soul and liberation from all passion and carnal desire that necessitates the cultivation of the virtues and the traversing of the spiritual stations. Had the soul not been separated from the Spirit by the veil of passion and ignorance, it would already have possessed the virtues and not been in any need of cultivating them. But precisely because the veil is there separating the soul from the light of the Spirit, which alone can enable it to gain direct knowledge of God, there must be spiritual discipline and a death and resurrection of the

[5] *Ibid.*, p. 171.
[6] *Tadhkirat al-awliyā'*, Part II, pp. 54–5.

soul so that it will become adorned with the virtues, thus making it worthy of the Divine Presence.

In the *Maḥāsin al-majālis*, which contains one of the most profound discussions of the spiritual virtues to be found in Sufism, the Moroccan Sufi Ibn al-'Arīf writes,

'If there had not been the darkness of separative existence, surely the light of the unseen would have become manifest. If there had not been the temptation of the carnal soul, it is certain that the veil would have been lifted. If there had not been causes of a created nature, the Divine Omnipotence would have emerged into full light. If there had not been any hypocrisy, gnosis would have been pure. If there had not been avidity, surely the love of God would have become firmly rooted [in the soul]. If some earthly pleasures had not remained, certainly the fire of the passionate love of God would have consumed the spirits [of men]. If the servant had ceased to be, the Lord would be contemplated. So when the veils are uplifted through the interruption of these partial causes and the obstacles are overcome through the amputation of these earthly attachments, there arrives what has already been said [by Ḥallāj]:

'A secret has been revealed to thee which for a long time had been hidden from thee; an aurora has shined of which thou art the obscurity.

'Thou art the veil which hides from thine heart the secret of His mystery; for without thee a seal would never have been set upon thy heart [depriving thee of the vision of God].

'If thou becomest absent from thy heart, He will install Himself there, and His tents will become spread on the highland of the well-guarded revelation.

'And there will be created a divine narrative whose audition is never wearisome and whose prose and poetry will become intensely desirable.'[7]

The journey upon the spiritual path is filled with ever-recurring encounters between the soul and the Spirit, some transient and some permanent, until the wild and unruly steed of the soul is disciplined and saddled and the soul becomes imbued with the fragrance of the Spirit, leading to the transformation of its own substance. The Sufis distinguish among the experiences of the soul upon the Path between

[7] Ibn al-'Arīf, *Maḥāsin al-majālis*, ed. and trans. into French by M. Asin Palacios, Paris, 1933, p. 76 of the Arabic text. The English translation is our own based on the Arabic text established by the editor.

permanent and passing states, calling the first *maqām* (pl. *maqāmāt*) or technically 'station' and the second *ḥāl* (pl. *aḥwāl*) or technically 'state'. The discussion of the spiritual states in the general sense of the term in Sufism is concerned essentially with the *aḥwāl* and *maqāmāt*, which of course, for reasons mentioned above, are inseparable from the virtues. A man who has not as yet felt the divine attraction and has not entered the spiritual path consoles himself with the world of multiplicity and usually knows nothing of the spiritual states. As Niffarī says, 'When I [God] am absent, gather to thyself thy misfortunes, and every phenomenal existence will come to console thee for My absence. If thou listenest, thou wilt obey; and if thou obeyest, thou wilt not see Me.'[8] But once by the grace of God the divine attraction (*jadhb*) comes and the soul begins to practice the spiritual discipline provided by Sufism, man begins to undergo those experiences which comprise the states (*aḥwāl*) and stations (*maqāmāt*).

The Sufis have discussed extensively the question of the *aḥwāl* and *maqāmāt* and the differences between them. And because each has spoken from a particular *maqām* himself, according to the verse of Shabistarī in his *Gulshan-i rāz*,

> As for the saints on this road before and behind
> They each give news of their own stages. . . .
> Since the language of each is according to his degree of progress,
> They are hard to be understood by the people[9]

outwardly their words differ although the inner meaning of all their sayings converges upon the same ineffable reality.

Classical texts of Sufism abound in technical definitions of *ḥāl* and *maqām* and the basic differences between them. The term *ḥāl* is sometimes used to mean state of soul[10] or mode of being in general. Ghazzālī in his *Iḥyā' 'ulūm al-dīn* uses it in the technical sense as the state of soul of the person who is practising Sufism and travelling on the Way. He writes, 'All the religious stations are composed of three

[8] A. J. Arberry, *The Mawāqif and Mukhāṭabāt of Niffarī*, London, 1935, p. 39.

[9] *The Mystic Rose Garden*, p. 3.

درین ره اولیاء بازازپس وپیش   نشا نی داده اند ازمنزل خویش
سنخها چون بوفق منزل افتاد   درافهام خلایق مشکل افتاد

[10] Ghazzālī uses it in the phrase 'pay attention to certain of his states of the soul' (الالتفات الى بعض احوال نفسه). *Al-I'tiqād fi'l-iqtiṣād*, Ankara, 1962, p. 166; see also F. Jabre, *Essai sur le lexique de Ghazali*, Beirut, 1970, p. 79, where the different usages of the term *ḥāl* by Ghazzālī are assembled.

elements: divine knowledge, states of the soul (*aḥwāl*) and acts.'[11] Most authors have defined *ḥāl* in conjunction and in contrast with *maqām*, so that Ghazzālī writes further on in the *Iḥyā'* that 'Qualification (*waṣf*) is called "station" (*maqām*) if it is stable and endures and it is called "state of soul" (*ḥāl*) if it passes away and disappears without delay. . . . What is not stable is called "state of soul" because it disappears to give its place to another [state] rapidly. This is true of all the qualifications of the heart.'[12]

In his famous *al-Ta'rīfāt* Jurjānī makes a similar distinction, and also he emphasizes the effort needed to acquire a *maqām* and the character of *ḥāl* as a gift from God: '*Ḥāl* among the "people of the Truth" (*ahl al-ḥaqq*) [the Sufis] is a spiritual meaning that is echoed in the heart without affectation. It is not earned or acquired, whether it be happiness or sadness, contraction or expansion or composure. It ceases with the appearance of the attributes of the carnal soul whether the like of it follows or not. . . . The *aḥwāl* are gifts from God while the *maqāmāt* are acquired. The *aḥwāl* come from the spring of divine generosity and the *maqāmāt* are achieved through the exertion of effort.'[13]

This distinction becomes more clear in the description of *ḥāl* and *maqām* given by Hujwīrī, the early authority on Sufism, in his *Kashf al-maḥjūb*. He writes,

'Station (*maqām*) denotes anyone's "standing" in the Way of God, and his fulfilment of the obligations appertaining to that "station" and his keeping it until he comprehends its perfection so far as lies in a man's power. It is not permissible that he should quit his "station" without fulfilling the obligations thereof. Thus, the first "station" is repentance (*tawbat*), then comes conversion (*inābat*), then renunciation (*zuhd*), then trust in God (*tawakkul*) and so on: it is not permissible that anyone should pretend to conversion without repentance, or to renunciation without conversion, or to trust in God without renunciation.

'State (*ḥāl*), on the other hand, is something that decends from God into a man's heart, without his being able to repel it when it

[11] '«وجميع مقامات الدّين انّماتنتظم من ثلاثة امور، معارف واحوال واعمال»' *Iḥyā' 'ulūm al-dīn*, Cairo, vol. IV, 1352/1933, p. 55; Jabre, *op. cit.*, p. 79.

[12] «انّما يسمّى الوصف مقاماً اذا ثبت واقام وانما يسمّى حالًا اذا كان عارضاً سريع الزوال . . . . . فالذى هوغيرثابت يسمى حالا لانّه يحول على القرب. وهذاجاز فى كل وصف من اوصاف القلب» *Iḥyā'*, vol. IV, p. 123.

[13] Mīr Sayyid Sharīf Jurjānī, *al-Ta'rīfāt*, Cairo, 1321 (A. H. Lunar), p. 56.

comes, or to attract it when it goes, by his own effort. Accordingly, while the term "station" denotes the way of the seeker, and his prayers in the field of exertion, and his rank before God in proportion to his merit, the term "state" denotes the favour and grace which God bestows upon the heart of His servant, and which are not connected with any mortification on the latter's part. "Station" belongs to the category of acts, "state" to the category of gifts. Hence the man that has a "station" stands by his own self-mortification, whereas the man that has a "state" is dead to "self" and stands by a "state" which God creates in him.'[14]

Most Sufis have accepted this major distinction between the two types of spiritual experience or state that the soul tastes in its spiritual journey, although a few like Ḥārith al-Muḥāsibī believed in the possibility of the permanence of *ḥāl* as well as *maqām*. The passing character of *ḥāl* as emphasized by most Sufis, however, denotes a profound reality that must be considered in any full exposition of the spiritual life. As a result of spiritual discipline the adept can gain a station (*maqām*) which is permanent, as seen above, in the sense that the disciple ascends in the scale of being to a new level of both existence and consciousness. To possess a *maqām* is an exalted position and not all aspirants within a Sufi order reach such a condition.

But because God is merciful and generous, He bestows upon the disciple through the channel of these very qualities an occasional spark of the divine light which for a moment illuminates his soul and puts him in a state beyond himself. A *ḥāl* is a divine gift which can come both to the beginner upon the Path and to the most advanced Sufi possessing a high station. In fact occasionally it can also come to the uninitiated if he be spiritually disposed to the reception of the grace of Heaven. The divine grace (*barakah*) flows too strongly in the arteries of the Universe not to touch occasionally even men who are not following the Way. The expansion of the soul and the sense of joy it experiences in seeing a beautiful face or hearing a lovely melody, which in their own way break the "contracting" influence of the cosmic environment upon the soul, foreshadow the *ḥāl* of those travelling upon the Path. That is why in both Arabic and Persian the term *ḥāl* has come to acquire a meaning wider than its strictly Sufi definition, that of an unusual and at the same time positive experience of the soul which brings it for a moment outside of its usual confines. But this secondary meaning itself reveals the profound nexus which

[14] R. A. Nicholson, *The Kashf al-Maḥjūb, the Oldest Persian Treatise on Sufism by 'Alī b. 'Uthmān al-Jullābī al-Hujwīrī*, London, 1911, p. 181.

binds the soul of man and even the man who has not taken the conscious step to devote himself to the Way, to the *barakah* flowing within the cosmos and of course even more to the world of the Spirit, which remains accessible to man as long as he remains in the human state.

The passing character of the *ḥāl*, however, indicates the necessity of persistence and continuous effort until man reaches the *maqām* of permanent proximity. Until that *maqām* is reached even the Sufi, or more correctly the *faqīr* or *darwīsh*, can always have a *ḥāl* which causes him to transcend his usual state of being. The poet Sa'dī in his *Gulistān* summarizes the character of *ḥāl* beautifully when he writes,

> One asked the man who had lost his son [a reference to the story of Jacob and Joseph as related in the Quran]:
> 'O noble and intelligent old man!
> As thou hast smelt the odour of his garment from Egypt
> Why has thou not seen him in the well of Canaan?' He replied:
> 'My state [*ḥāl*] is that of leaping lightning.
> One moment it appears and at another vanishes.
> I am sometimes sitting in high heaven.
> Sometimes I cannot see the back of my foot.
> Were a dervish always to remain in that state
> He would not care for the two worlds.'[15]

In contrast to the fleeting nature of *ḥāl* the permanence of *maqām* implies that it can be surpassed only when it is fully possessed and all of its conditions are fulfilled. Moreover, to reach a higher *maqām* means to continue to possess the *maqām* below, not to become deprived of it. The *maqāmāt* are in reality so many states of being or degrees of consciousness leading to union, and they stand related to each other in a hierarchical order so that even when transcended they remain a permanent possession of the seeker who has passed through them. Moreover, to possess a *maqām* means not only to experience it

[15] Sa'dī, *The Gulistan or Rose Garden*, trans. by E. Rahatsek, London, 1964, p. 120.

یکی پرسید از آن گم گشته فرزند — که ای روشن گهر پیر خردمند
زمصرش بوی پیراهن شنیدی — چرادر چاه کنعانش ندیدی
بگفت احوال ما برق جها نست — دمی پیدا و دیگر دم نهانست
گهی بر طارم اعلی نشینم — گهی بر پشت پای خودنبینم
اگر درویش درحالی بماندی — سر دست از دوعالم برفشاندی

outwardly, but also to be wholly transformed by it and, as mentioned already, in a sense to *be* that *maqām*. Concerning truthfulness (*ṣidq*), which is one of the highest *maqāmāt* and in a sense the crown of all virtues,[16] the Sufi Abū Sa'īd al-Kharrāz writes,

'In this way his characteristics and states change and become easy for him, and out of every station which he endures and suffers for God's sake, seeking His favour, he gets a like recompense of good. So his character changes and his intellect revives: the light of truth lodges in him, and he grows familiar with it; evil desire flees him, and its darkness is extinguished. Then it is that truthfulness and its characteristics become part of his nature: nothing but this finds he good, and with this only he associates, for he is content with naught else.'[17]

When it comes to an actual description of the *aḥwâl* and *maqāmāt*, there are many ways in which the Sufis have described these steps leading from man to God. Especially in the case of the *aḥwāl* it is hardly possible to limit them to a set number. In one of the earliest authoritative texts of Sufism, the *Kitāb al-luma'*, Abû Naṣr al-Sarrāj enumerates ten states of the soul (*aḥwāl*): constant attention (*murāqabah*), proximity (*qurb*), love (*maḥabbah*), fear (*khawf*), hope (*rajā'*), spiritual yearning (*shawq*), familiarity (*uns*), tranquility (*iṭmi'nān*), contemplation (*mushāhadah*) and certainty (*yaqīn*).[18] But inasmuch as a *ḥāl* is a divine gift it can take on many forms and colours and as already mentioned its kinds are hardly enumerable. The above are most certainly to be considered among the basic states, although some of them can also become permanent, so that certain of the later Sufis have included some of these *aḥwāl* as *maqāmāt*. The journey of the soul towards God includes too many imponderable elements to allow it to be reduced to a set scheme. All schemes in fact are only an aid for the soul on its journey. One must actually be there to know all the states and stations involved in the traversing of the Way.

By nature of their permanence and stability the stations are somewhat easier than the states to enumerate, although here also there are numerous ways of describing the steps that separate man from God.

[16] The spiritual virtues have been discussed in a masterly way by F. Schuon under the three cardinal virtues of humility, charity and truthfulness in his *Spiritual Perspectives and Human Facts*.

[17] Abū Sa'īd al-Kharrāz, *The Book of Truthfulness* (*Kitāb al-Ṣidq*), ed. and trans. by A. J. Arberry, London, 1937, p. 51.

[18] Abū Naṣr al-Sarrāj, *Kitāb al-luma'*, ed. by R. A. Nicholson, Leyden, 1914, p. 42.

It is like wanting to describe the number of steps that must be taken to climb a mountain. The beginning and end are known as well as the major features on the way. But the actual number and the details of each step depend on the climber as well as on the path and its beginning and end. The *Kitāb al-luma'* mentions seven *maqāmāt* that have become famous in later Sufism and include repentance (*tawbah*), abstention (*wara'*), asceticism (*zuhd*), poverty (*faqr*), patience (*ṣabr*), confidence (*tawakkul*) and contentment (*riḍā'*).[19] Other Sufis like 'Alā' al-Dawlah Simnānī have described the *maqāmāt* in terms of the 'seven prophets' of one's inner being, with each prophet corresponding to one of man's inner states and also virtues.[20] Yet others like Khwājah 'Abdallāh Anṣārī have gone into great detail in dividing the stages of man's ascent to God into a hundred stations.[21] But through all these descriptions the main features of the stations marking the journey toward God are the same.

One of the earliest and finest accounts of the *maqāmāt* in Sufism is the *Forty Stations* (*Maqāmāt-i arba'īn*) of the fifth/eleventh-century Sufi master Abū Sa'īd ibn Abi'l-Khayr, already known to the West for his remarkable quatrains.[22] The original text of the *Forty Stations* has been recently edited for the first time.[23] Because of the importance of this early text and also its simplicity, beauty and clarity, we give a complete translation of it below in order to make possible a direct

[19] *Ibid.* Following al-Sarrāj many Sufis have enumerated seven stages as the fundamental stages of the spiritual path. 'Aṭṭār thus speaks of the seven cities of love (*haft shahr-i 'ishq*) and Aḥmad Ghazzālī mentions in his *Baḥr al-ḥaqīqah* that man must cross seven seas in order to reach *fanâ'*.

[20] H. Corbin, 'Physiologie de l'homme de lumière dans le soufisme iranien,' *Ombre et Lumière*, Paris, 1959, pp. 238 ff.

[21] This has been done in his *Hundred Fields of Spiritual Combat* (*Ṣad maydān*); see S. de Beaurecueil, 'Une ébauche persane des "Manāzil as-Sā'irīn": le "Kitāb-é Ṣad Maydān" de 'Abdallāh Anṣārī,' *Mélanges islamologiques*, vol. II, Cairo, 1954, pp. 1–90; also *Ṣad maydān*, ed. by 'A. Ḥabībī, Kabul, 1341 (A. H. Solar).

[22] See R. A. Nicholson, *Studies in Islamic Mysticism*, Cambridge, 1919, chapter I.

[23] See M. Dāmādī, 'Maqāmāt-i arba'īn-i Abū Sa'īd,' *Ma'ārif-i islāmī* (*Islamic Culture*), vol. XII, April 1971, pp. 58–62. The edition is based on the Aya Sophia ms. 4819. See also Danechpazhuh, *Fihrist-i mīkrawfīlmhā-yi kitābkhānah-i markazī-yi Dānishgāh-i Tihrān*, Tehran, 1348 (A. H. Solar), p. 416. After the publication of Dāmādī's text and our translation of it, a Pakistani scholar, Professor Riāḍ Khān, has informed us that there are several excellent manuscripts of this work in the libraries of the sub-continent of which most are attributed to Mīr Sayyid 'Alī Hamadānī. Be it as it may, the identity of the author does not change in any way the innate quality of this text and its importance for an understanding of the *aḥwāl* and *maqāmāt* in Sufism.

taste of the description of the *maqāmāt* as given by one of the great Sufi masters themselves:[24]

'In the Name of Allah Most Merciful and Compassionate
'And in Him is our refuge.

'The Shaykh, the traveller upon the spiritual path, the devotee of God, the king of the saints among those who have inquired into the Truth, Abū Sa'īd ibn Abi'l-Khayr, may Allah illuminate his spirit, has said that the Sufi must possess forty stations (*maqāmāt*) if his march upon the path of Sufism is to be acceptable.

'The first station is intention (*niyyat*). The Sufi must possess such an intention that if he were to be given this world and its blessings and the other world and its paradise or its calamity and affliction, he would give away this world and its blessings to the infidels, the other world and its paradise to the believers and keep the calamity and affliction for himself.

'The second station is conversion (*inābat*). If he is in spiritual solitude (*khalwat*) he sees God. Changes in the world do not alter his inner secret and calamities sent by Heaven do not cause the bird of his love to fly away.

'The third station is repentence (*tawbat*). All men repent from what is forbidden (*ḥarām*) and do not eat of the forbidden lest they suffer punishment. They [the Sufis] repent from what is lawful (*ḥalāl*) and eat of what is lawful lest they become afflicted by what is forbidden and doubtful.

'The fourth station is discipleship (*irādat*). All men seek comfort and with it wealth and worldly blessings. They seek affliction and with it dominion and sanctity.

'The fifth station is spiritual struggle (*mujāhadat*). People seek to multiply ten into twenty. They try to turn twenty into nothing.

'The sixth station is constant attention (*murāqabat*). Constant attention is to guard one's soul in spiritual retreat until of necessity the Lord of the Universe preserves one from committing sin.

'The seventh station is patience (*ṣabr*). If the disaster of the two worlds befalls them they will not so much as sigh. And if the love of the people of the world descends upon them they will not cease to march on the path of patience.

'The eighth station is invocation (*dhikr*). In their heart they know

[24] The present translation is based on the text established by Dāmādī with a few corrections made by the author where it was felt that the implied meaning required another reading of the text. The *Maqāmāt* of Abū Sa'īd recall those given by Qushayrī in his famous *Risālah* and resemble them in many ways. See A. J. Arberry, *Sufism*, London, 1953, chapter VII.

Him and with their tongue they invoke Him. Whenever they are in an impasse they know no road save that which leads to His Presence.

'The ninth station is contentment (*riḍā*). If they are kept without clothing [by God] they are happy and if they are kept hungry they are happy. Never do they reside in the house of self-will.

'The tenth station is opposition to the carnal soul (*mukhālafat-i nafs*). For seventy years their carnal soul cries in agony with the desire of receiving a single favour and does not receive anything but pain and hardship.

'The eleventh station is agreement (*muwāfaqat*). Disaster and well-being, favour and privation are the same for them.

'The twelfth station is surrender (*taslīm*). If the arrow of fate faces them from the hiding place of calamity they place themselves in the catapult of surrender and open themselves before the arrow of fate, making their soul and heart a shield before it. In front of the arrow of fate they stand still.

'The thirteenth station is confidence (*tawakkul*). They do not demand anything of creatures nor of God. They worship Him only for Himself. There are no questions or answers exchanged. Consequently the Lord of the Universe enables them to attain the object of their desire when they are in need, and there is no reckoning involved.

'The fourteenth station is asceticism (*zuhd*). From all the wealth of this world they have only a patched cloak of a hundred pieces made of muslin, a mat and a piece of felt. That cloak is a thousand times dearer to them than fine scarlet cloth and sumptuous dress.

'The fifteenth station is worship (*'ibādat*). Throughout the day they are occupied with the reading of the Quran and the invocation of the Name of God and throughout the night they remain standing on their feet. Their bodies are seeking to be of service, their hearts are exuberant with the love of the One, their heads are roaring in quest of the contemplation of the King.

'The sixteenth station is abstention (*wara'*). They do not eat of just any food, nor do they wear just any kind of clothing. They do not sit in the company of just any kind of people and they do not choose the companionship of anyone save God, exalted be He.

'The seventeenth station is sincerity (*ikhlāṣ*). Throughout the night they pray and throughout the day they fast. If their carnal soul does not obey and then they observe obedience, they will sell fifty years of obedience for the drinking of a sip of water and give those fifty years to a dog or to whomever it might be. Then they will say, "O soul! Dost thou now understand that what thou didst is not becoming of God?"

'The eighteenth station is truthfulness (*ṣidq*). They do not take a single step without truthfulness and do not breathe a single breath save in truth. Their tongues speak of their hearts and their hearts of their inner secrets and their inner secrets of God.

'The nineteenth station is fear (*khawf*). When they look at His justice they melt in fear, and they have no hope in being obedient [towards God's commands].

'The twentieth station is hope (*rajā*). When they regard His grace they boast in joy, and they have no fear or terror.

'The twenty-first station is annihilation (*fanā*). They melt their carnal souls in the crucible of annihilation and become annihilated from all that is below Him. Their tongues do not speak of things of this world. There is nothing upon their tongues save His Name. Their bodies do not move save to obey Him and their minds do not spring into action save for Him.

'The twenty-second station is subsistence (*baqā*). If they look to the right they see God and if they look to the left they see God. They see Him in whatever condition they are. They subsist through His subsistence. They are satisfied with what He has ordained for them. They are joyous because of His grace and bounty.

'The twenty-third station is the science of certainty (*'ilm al-yaqīn*). When they look through the eye of the science of certainty they see from the highest heavens to the lowest level of the earth without any veil.

'The twenty-fourth station is the truth of certainty (*ḥaqq al-yaqīn*). When they see through the eye of the truth of certainty they pass beyond all artifacts and creatures and see God without any hows and whys and without any veil.

'The twenty-fifth station is gnosis (*ma'rifat*). Through all the creatures of the two worlds and through all people they perceive God, and there is no accusation to be made of their perception.

'The twenty-sixth station is effort (*jahd*). They worship Him in their hearts and in their souls, and there is no doubt in their obedience.

'The twenty-seventh station is sanctity (*wilāyat*). This world and the next are not fit to be embraced by their spiritual will (*himmat*), and all of paradise and its bounties are not worth an atom in their eyes.

'The twenty-eighth station is love (*maḥabbat*). Throughout the whole world they have only one Friend. Their love is one, for both outwardly and inwardly they are with the One. Their bodies melt in joy and their hearts are always happy in the Sacred Presence. They have no thought of children or wife, of the world or of wealth.

'The twenty-ninth station is ecstacy (*wajd*). They are not to be found in the world, nor in the graveyard nor at the Resurrection nor on the straight path (*ṣirāṭ*) [bridging over hell and leading to Heaven]. They are in the Most Sublime Presence. Where they reside there is only God and them.

'The thirtieth station is proximity (*qurb*). If they say, "O God! Make all the people of infidelity and rebellion and all the people of polytheism and revolt be forgiven because of us," the Lord of the Universe will not reject their demand.

'The thirty-first station is meditation (*tafakkur*). Their intimate friend is His Name. Their peace resides in His message.

'The thirty-second station is union (*wiṣāl*). Although their person is in this world, their heart is with the Lord.

'The thirty-third station is unveiling (*kashf*). There is no veil between God and their hearts. If they look below they will see as far as the *Gāw-māhī* [the creature supporting the earth].[25] And if they look above they will see the Throne and the Pedestal, the Pen and the Guarded Tablet as far as the Sacred Precinct (*haḍīrat al-quds*). Nothing is hidden from them.

'The thirty-fourth station is service (*khidmat*). They do not cease to render service for the blinking of an eye. Nor are they for a single moment absent from the presence of the Friend.

'The thirty-fifth station is catharsis (*tajrīd*). If they be taken to hell, they say "Greetings!", and if they be taken to paradise, they say "Greetings!" Neither does paradise cause them joy nor hell fear. They never turn away from His friendship and they possess nothing of all that is in this world.

'The thirty-sixth station is aloneness (*tafrīd*). In this world they are strangers among creatures. If they be beaten they will not leave the Path and if they be caressed they will not be fooled.

'The thirty-seventh station is expansion (*inbisāṭ*). They are audacious before God. If the Lord of the Universe sends the angel of death to them at the time of death, they will not obey. Until they hear from the Friend of the world they will not allow their souls to depart. They do not fear Nakīr and Munkar [the angels who question the dead in the grave] and they do not give a thought to the Resurrection. They neither set foot in the Supreme Heaven nor look upon the face of the houris and the heavenly mansions until they have had a vision of the forgiving King.

'The thirty-eighth station is the ascertaining of the Truth (*taḥqīq*).

[25] The *Gāw-māhī* is a mythical creature, half fish and half bull, which supports the earth.

They are all in a state of wonder with cries and lamentation. They flee from creatures and hang by the chain of His gate.

'The thirty-ninth station is the supreme goal (*nihāyat*). They have reached the inn by the roadside and have cut through the deserts of calamity. With the eye of the heart they have seen God.

'The fortieth station is Sufism (*taṣawwuf*). The Sufi is he who has become purified of all desire. His inner being is purified from wretchedness. His words are free from inadvertancy, thoughtlessness and calumny. His mind is radiant and his eyes are turned away from the world. He has become instructed with the Truth.

'Of these stations, each belongs to a prophet among the prophets—may peace be upon them—the first Adam and the last Muḥammad—upon them and upon other prophets and messengers and the angels of proximity be peace. And may God, the Exalted, be satisfied with all the companions of His Prophet. Amen.'

As is seen in this description of the spiritual stations, Abū Sa'īd includes certain of the *aḥwāl* of other Sufis as *maqāmāt*, and also he includes other stations after *baqā'*, which is usually considered as the highest station since it is that of union with God. But the stations that follow may be said to be so many stations in the journey *in* God (*fi'llāh*) after the traveller has ended the journey *to* God (*ila'llāh*). Even the station of service (*khidmat*) that comes after *baqā'* must not be considered as action or religious service in the usual sense of the word but as service rendered by a being who has already tasted of union with God (*wiṣāl*). In its own order it is something analogous to the vow of Avalokiteśvāra in Buddhism to save all creatures after having already set one foot in *nirvana*.[26]

The highest station described by Abū Sa'īd is Sufism itself. For to have reached Sufism in its fullness or to be a Sufi in the true sense of the word is to have experienced all the stations and at the same time to have passed beyond all of them to the Supreme Station of the full realization of Unity (*tawḥīd*), which is the end of the spiritual life in Islam as in other authentic traditions. Between the station of the Sufi and the man who is spiritually asleep but who considers this death or state of negligence as normal there stand all the spiritual stations and states, the experience of any one of which would cause the most intense worldly experience of the soul to pale into insignificance. The experience of these states remains a possibility for any man who is willing to devote himself fully to the spiritual life and who

[26] See F. Schuon, *In the Tracks of Buddhism*, trans. by M. Pallis, London, 1968, chapter XV.

seeks these states and stations with the correct intention—not as ends in themselves but as steps that lead to the One who is above and beyond all states and stations of the soul and who resides at the same time at the centre of man's being at the origin of the axis which unites all the states of man's being, the corporeal, the psychic and the spiritual, with their common Principle.

VI

Man in the Universe: Permanence Amidst Apparent Change

One of the questions that lies at the heart of Sufi teachings is the situation of man in the Universe, for it is from this situation that man must of necessity begin the spiritual journey which will finally lead him beyond the cosmos. And it is precisely the deformation of the true image of the situation of man in the Universe during the past few centuries in the West, especially with the rise of the evolutionist theories, that has caused many dazzlingly clear spiritual verities to appear improbable. To understand fully the teachings of Sufism, it is therefore necessary to examine once again the relation of man to the world that surrounds him in the light of the question of change and permanence, removing in this manner the obstacles that impede one's full understanding of the reality that surrounds man and determines his further becoming.

In the perspective of the modern world there is no sphere in which change and transformation reign with the same supremacy and totality as in that which concerns nature and man's relation to it and knowledge of it. Modern science, which has acted as a catalyst during the past centuries for change in so many other fields, is itself based upon change and impermanence; were it to cease to change and become immutable it would cease to exist in its present form. Moreover, since this is the only science of nature known to modern man, the whole relation between man and nature, as well as the nature of man himself and the Universe that surrounds him, is seen only in the light of flux and change. The view that man's position in the Universe and his knowledge of it, not to speak of the object of this knowledge, is constantly changing has come to be regarded as so self-evident as to make any other point of view appear absurd and well-nigh unintelligible for those whose knowledge is limited to the horizons of the modern world. Contemporary man is bewildered at even the possibility of an element of permanence in his relation with the Universe, not because such an element does not exist, but because the problem is never considered from the point of view of permanence.

It is often forgotten that before man began to view his relation to nature only from the aspect of change and evolution he had become himself inwardly detached from the immutable principle of the Intellect, the *nous*, which, along with revelation, is the only factor that can act as the permanent and immutable axis for the machinations of human reason. With the weakening of intellectual and gnostic elements in Christianity (if we understand by gnosis that illuminative knowledge which Sufism calls *'irfân* and which is the very heart of Sufism as of every authentic and complete spiritual tradition), the rational faculty of Western man became gradually estranged from the twin sources of all immutability, stability and permanence: namely, revelation and intellectual intuition.[1] The result was on the one hand the nominalist trend, which destroyed philosophical certainty, and on the other this reduction of man to his narrowly human aspects, cut off from any transcendental elements; such is the man of Renaissance humanism. This way of conceiving man itself implied his total involvement in sheer change and becoming; this effect can be seen even outwardly during that period in the rapid transformations in Western society which have given the Renaissance its transitional character. But even then man's concept of the Universe had not as yet changed. His science of nature was still essentially medieval, comprised of Hermetic and Scholastic elements. First of all it was only his conception of himself that changed, leading in its turn by degrees to a change in his concept of the Universe and his own place in it.

It is always important to bear in mind the time lag between the religious and metaphysical revolt at the end of the Middle Ages in the Occident, which expresses an attempt on the part of Western man to cut himself away from his celestial and immutable archetype and to become purely terrestrial and human, and the scientific revolution which carried this secularized vision of man to its logical conclusion by creating a purely secular science. Western man, who during the Renaissance considered himself a secular being, began to develop a science that considered the changing aspect of things alone, a science that was concerned solely with becoming rather than being. And this is a most logical happening if we remember that even etymologically *secular* is derived from the Latin *saecularis* one of whose meanings is change and temporality. The destruction of the sacred vision of man and the Universe is equivalent to the destruction of the immutable aspect of both man and the Universe. A secular science could not have come into existence without being wholly concerned with change and becoming.

[1] See S. H. Nasr, *The Encounter of Man and Nature, the Spiritual Crisis of Modern Man*, London, 1968, pp. 63 ff.

If we keep in mind the historical factors that brought into being a world view in the West which is based solely on the changing aspect of things, it should be possible for us to reconstruct and bring back to light in the vision of modern man the long overlooked permanent elements without appearing to speak of absurdities. But this can only happen if there is an understanding of traditional metaphysics and the language of symbolism through which the metaphysical truths have always been revealed.[2] Metaphysics, or the science of the permanent, which is the basic element of Sufi doctrine, can be ignored or forgotten; but it cannot be refuted, precisely because it is immutable and not related to change *qua* change. That which deals with permanence cannot become 'out of date', because it is not concerned with any date as such. The permanent elements in the relation between man and the Universe remain as valid now as ever. Only they must become known once again in the West after the long period during which Western man did not search for permanent elements within change itself and even sought to reduce permanence itself to change and historical process. In the traditional circles of the East, but of course not among modernized classes obsessed with Westernization, this aspect of permanence has never been forgotten or lost sight of because the sense of the sacred, hence of the immutable, has continued to dominate all of life.

From the point of view of traditional metaphysical and cosmological doctrines there are several elements of permanence in the relationship between man and nature and in his situation in the Universe. The first and the most basic element is that the cosmic environment that surrounds man is not ultimate reality but possesses the character of relativity and even of illusion. If one understands what is meant by the Absolute (*muṭlaq*) then by the same token one understands the relative (*muqayyad*) and comes to realize that all that is not Absolute must of necessity be relative.

The aspect of the world as veil (*ḥijāb*) in the language of Sufism or as *maya* to use the Hindu term or again as *samsara* in the Buddhist sense is itself a permanent element of the cosmos and man's relation to it. The Universe, in its cosmic aspect, was always *maya* and will always be *maya*. The Absolute is always the Absolute and the relative the relative, and no amount of historical process and change can turn the one into the other. Historical process can cause a people or even a whole civilization to forget for a while the distinction between the Absolute and the relative and therefore to take the relative for the

[2] See F. Schuon, *The Transcendent Unity of Religions*, pp. 9 ff., and R. Guénon, *La métaphysique orientale*, Paris, 1951.

Absolute, the created order (*al-khalq*) for the Uncreated Truth (*al-ḥaqq*), as modern science seems to have done. But wherever and whenever metaphysical discernment appears, the distinction becomes clear and the world becomes known for what it is, namely *maya*. The changing element of the world which the concept of *maya* implies is itself a permanent feature of the world. It is in the nature of the world to be changing, to undergo generation and corruption, to experience life and death. But the meaning of this change can only be understood in terms of the permanent. To have understood that the world is *maya* is to have understood the meaning of Atman or Brahman, which transcends *maya*. To know that the world is impermanent or *samsaric* in nature is to know by extension of the presence of the *nirvanic* state beyond it.[3] The very realization of the character of the world as *al-khalq* implies the awareness of *al-ḥaqq* which transcends it and at the same time shines through it.

The changing character of the world reveals metaphysically the permanent reality that transcends it. To realize the relativity of things is to know, by an extension of the same knowledge, of the Absolute and the Permanent. Throughout history, in all periods of human culture, this metaphysical distinction has existed. It lies in the nature of things and so is there for all to see provided they turn their vision towards it. Only, at certain times such as ours the relative has come to be idolized as the Absolute.

Today, one often hears the claim that all is relative. But the same people who make such a claim often bestow an absolute character upon the domain of the relative itself. Without always being fully aware of it, they mistake Brahman for *maya*, due to a lack of discernment and true knowledge, an ignorance which itself comes from *maya*. But when there is metaphysical knowledge there is also awareness of the relativity of things in the light of the Absolute, and this fundamental truth is a permanent element in man's situation in the Universe, and concerns his destiny as a being who is called upon to try and transcend the cosmic crypt into which he has fallen and to return from the domain of the relative to the Absolute.[4]

Another element of permanence in the relation of man to the Universe is the manifestation of the Absolute in the relative in the form of symbols (*rumûz*) understood in the traditional sense of the

[3] See F. Schuon, *In the Tracks of Buddhism*, trans. by M. Pallis, where the relation between *nirvana* and *samsara* is discussed in all its amplitude and depth.

[4] Concerning this theme in its Islamic setting, see S. H. Nasr, *An Introduction to Islamic Cosmological Doctrines*, chapter XV.

word.[5] The symbol is not based on man-made conventions. It is an aspect of the ontological reality of things and as such is independent of man's perception of it.[6] The symbol is the revelation of a higher order of reality in a lower order through which man can be led back to the higher realm. To understand symbols is to accept the hierarchic structure of the Universe and the multiple states of being.

During certain phases of historical process symbols which are given special significance and power in a revealed religion through the revelation itself can gradually lose their efficacy either partially or completely as a result of the weakening of the spiritual basis of that religion, as can be seen in the case of the 'de-mythologizers' of our day. But the symbols existing in nature are permanent and immutable. What the sky signifies symbolically, as for example the dimension of transcendence and the Divine throne (*al-'arsh*)—to use the Islamic image—is as permanent as the sky itself. As long as the sun shines it will symbolize the Universal Intellect; similarly the tree with its extended branches remains a symbol of the multiple states of being as long as trees grow on the surface of the earth. That is why one may speak of a perennial cosmology, a *cosmologia perennis*, of a qualitative science of nature which is always valid and which reveals an aspect of nature which is, to say the least, no less real than the changing aspect studied by modern science.[7]

The main difference between the traditional and modern sciences of nature lies in the fact that modern science studies change with respect to change, whereas traditional science studies change *vis-à-vis* permanence through the study of symbols, which are nothing but the reflections of permanence in the realm of change.

A civilization may develop a science which turns its back upon the qualitative aspect of things revealed through symbols in order to concentrate upon the changes which can be measured quantitatively. But it cannot destroy the symbolic reality of things any more than can a qualitative and symbolic study of natural phenomena destroy their

[5] The meaning of traditional symbols cannot be fully treated here. This question has been amply dealt with in the writings of F. Schuon, R. Guénon, T. Burckhardt and A. K. Coomaraswamy as well as H. Zimmer and M. Eliade.

[6] 'The science of symbols—not simply a knowledge of traditional symbols—proceeds from the qualitative significances of substances, forms. . . . we are not dealing here with subjective appreciations, for the cosmic qualities are ordered both in relation to Being and according to a hierarchy which is more real than the individual. . . .' F. Schuon, *Gnosis, Divine Wisdom*, trans. G. E. H. Palmer, London, 1959, p. 110.

[7] On the *cosmologia perennis*, see T. Burckhardt, *Scienza moderna e saggezza tradizionale*, Torino, 1968; see also his *Alchemie, Sinn und Weltbild*, Olten, 1960, which deals with permanent values of Hermetic cosmology.

weight or size. Today, through the destruction of the 'symbolist' spirit[8] in the West, men have lost the sense of penetrating into the inner meaning of phenomena, which symbols alone reveal. But this impotence does not mean that natural symbols have ceased to exist. The symbolic significance of the homocentric spheres of Ptolemaic astronomy, which the immediate appearance of the heavens reveals, remains valid whether in the theoretical Newtonian absolute space or the curved space of relativity the earth moves round the sun or the sun round the earth. The homocentric spheres symbolize states of being above the terrestial state in which man is presently placed. The states of being remain real whether we understand and accept the natural symbolism which the heavens themselves reveal to us in our immediate and direct contact with them or whether in the name of other theoretical considerations we disregard this immediate appearance and the symbol which this appearance conveys.

In fact, even new scientific theories, if they conform to any reality at all, possess their own symbolic meaning. To correspond to reality in any degree means to be symbolic. If the Ptolemaic spheres symbolize man's position with respect to higher states of being, the galactic space of modern astronomy itself symbolizes the indefinity of the relative, the vastness of the ocean of *samsara*. It is itself a proof of the fact that man's intelligence was created to know the Infinite rather than the indefinite. But in a more direct sense, the symbolic meaning of the phenomena of nature, not to mention scientific theories based upon them, represents a permanent aspect of things and of man's relation to the cosmos. It is upon this permanent character of the symbolic content of the phenomena of nature that one can construct a symbolic science of nature, a traditional cosmology which remains of perennial value and permanent importance, and which is of all the greater significance today when the purely quantitative sciences of nature and their application threaten the existence of both man and nature.[9]

Yet another permanent feature of the relation between man and the Universe, at least from a certain aspect of the situation, is the way that nature presents itself to man. Today modern man seeks to change all his social, political and even religious institutions with the excuse that nature itself is always changing and therefore man must change. In fact just the reverse holds true. It is because man's mentality has lost its anchor in the permanent and become itself a fleeting river of

[8] Concerning the 'symbolist spirit' see F. Schuon, 'The Symbolist Outlook' *Studies in Comparative Religion*, Winter, 1966, pp. 50 ff.

[9] The author has dealt fully with the question in his *Encounter of Man and Nature*.

ever changing ideas and images that man sees only change in nature. Modern man has read evolution into nature; he began to believe in evolution in his mind before he had ever observed it in nature. Evolution is not the product of natural observation but of a secularized mentality cut off from every avenue of access to the immutable, which then began to see its own fleeting nature in outward nature. Man always sees in nature the reflection of his own being and his conception of what he himself is.

If we study the world about us we see that in fact the terrestrial environment in which men saw permanence for millennia has not changed in its general features. The sun still rises and sets the same way now as it did for ancient and medieval man, who looked upon it as the symbol of the Divine Intellect. The natural forms still reproduce themselves with the same regularity and through the same processes as in older historical periods. Neither the petals of the rose nor its scent have changed since Dante and Shakespeare wrote about them. Nor in fact has man himself evolved biologically since there has been a recorded or even unrecorded human history. The men of today are biologically the same as the men of old who believed in permanence and transcendence. If modern men have ceased to so believe they had better find some other excuse than their own biological or natural evolution.

In this question of the permanence of natural phenomena as they appear to man there is a diametrical opposition between the traditional point of view and the modern one which is its complete inversion. Today all things are considered to be changing, yet the hypothesis of uniformitarianism is used with such certainty in geology, paleontology and even anthropology that one would think it is proven law. On the one hand it is said that laws have been uniform and so we speak of events having taken place millions and billions of years ago without considering exactly what it is that we mean by a 'million years'. On the other hand we say that nature changes all the time, without considering the possibility that what appears as a 'law of nature' today may itself have changed over the ages or under particular circumstances and conditions. If we cannot walk on water, there is no logical reason why such and such a prophet or saint could not have done so in ages past.

The traditional view of nature reverses this situation completely. In place of change it substitutes permanence and in place of uniformity and immutability of natural conditions, qualitative change. The changing processes of nature are viewed as permanent patterns which through repetition integrate time and process into the image of eternity.[10] The apparent uniformity of nature is in turn modified by the theory of cycles, the *yugas* of Hinduism or *al-adwâr* and *al-akwâr* of certain schools of Islamic cosmology, by which is not meant mere repetition of the same patterns but rather the qualitative differences which exist between different epochs both in the cosmos and in human history. The modern inversion of these two realities has destroyed the vision of permanence in nature as well as the realization of the qualitative differences in various cycles. In fact this inversion is itself proof of the reality of the cosmic cycles and only confirms what all authentic traditions teach about them and particularly about the period in which we now are living.[11]

For this reason alone older works of natural history and mythology have become closed books and at best are interpreted in a purely psychological manner whereas they can be understood in the light of the fact that there is a qualitative difference in the cosmic medium of the ancient natural environment and our own. There was not then the same crystallization and condensation, the same separation of matter from the spirit as now. The water of Thales was still full of the animating spirit of nature and in fact symbolized the psycho-physical substratum of things. It was very far removed from the post-Cartesian dead matter with which Lavoisier was experimenting twenty-four centuries later.

Yet between this change and permanence and amidst this inversion of views there remains one immutable element; that is, the way in which the phenomena of nature appear to man. The sky, the sea, the mountains, the seasonal cycles, these realities manifest themselves now just as they did in the millennia before (certain qualitative differences apart), and they are the majestic testament of the Immutable manifested in the process of becoming. Men who love nature are essentially in quest of the permanent, and nature in fact itself gives the lie to those who want to limit all reality to change and becoming. Philosophies which are limited to the relative alone never arose among people who lived close to nature but have always been the products of sedentary ways of life where an artificial environment has enabled

[10] On the relation between linear and cyclic time as it affects both history and cosmology, see M. Eliade, *The Myth of the Eternal Return*, trans. by W. Trask, New York, 1954; see also, A. K. Coomaraswamy, *Time and Eternity*, Ascona, 1947, where the metaphysical relationship between time and eternity in different traditions is elucidated.

[11] The downward tendency of the *Kali Yuga*, which itself obliterates the vision of qualitative time for most men, is treated admirably by R. Guénon in many of his writings, especially *The Reign of Quantity and the Signs of the Times*, trans. by Lord Northbourne, London, 1956.

men to forget both nature and the permanent elements which it reveals to man, elements that evoke in the mind of man those permanent factors that are anchored in the immutable strata of his own being.

As far as the modern sciences of nature are concerned, with all the differences that distinguish them from the various traditional cosmologies, even here there is an element of permanence if one takes modern science for what it really is. Of course by the very fact that the latter has consciously turned its back upon the metaphysical and symbolic aspect of things, it is cut off from the traditional view of nature through its own point of view and is caused to ignore any metaphysical significance that its own discoveries may possess. Yet, these discoveries, to the extent that they have some connection with the reality of things, do possess a symbolic significance. For example the fact that order repeats itself in all planes of material reality from the galaxy to the atom, or the fact that whatever unit science deals with, whether it be the biological cell or the atom, there is a harmony of parts within a whole, represent permanent features of any science of nature irrespective of whether one bothers to take them into consideration or not.

In a still more evident manner, one observes the repetition of certain patterns and problems throughout the history of science, a fact which has attracted the attention of many modern scientists. No matter how much science changes, the encounter of man's mind with nature seems to produce certain permanent features. Take for example the problem of the continuity and discontinuity of bodies, which has occupied Aristotle and the Greek atomists, the Muslim Peripatetics and theologians as well as the modern physicists. Or the relation of the One to the manifold, or between order and disorder or between chance and determinism; these are all problems that recur perennially in all forms of science. Many scientists turn today to the history of science to find inspiration for new methodologies in order to face certain problems of contemporary physics or biology which are basically related to the problems of the ancient and medieval sciences. The recurrence of these patterns and problems in a field which is the most changing and fluid of all is yet another element of permanence in science itself despite the fact that it has turned its back upon Unity in order to study multiplicity and ignored the Principle while trying to analyze the contingent.

But perhaps the most important permanent element in man's relation to the Universe is his 'existential' situation in the hierarchy of universal existence (*marâtib al-wujûd*). Traditional man knew with certainty where he came from, why he lived and whither he was going.

The Holy Quran summarizes this certainty in these simple yet majestic words 'انّا للّه وإنّا إليه راجعون' 'Lo! we are Allah's and lo! unto Him we are returning' (II:156), and many treatises of Sufism and theosophy (*ḥikmah*) bear the title of 'the beginning and end' (*al-mabda' wa'l-ma'âd*), the *alpha* and *omega* which contains in summary fashion all truth and wisdom. Modern man, generally speaking, knows neither where he comes from nor what his end will be and therefore he does not know *why* he is living. But like the traditional man he faces the two points which determine the beginning and end of his terrestrial life. He is born and he dies. This fact has not changed one *iota* nor will it do so through recourse to some cheap form of immortality such as heart transplantation. The only difference is that what was once certainty has become today doubt and fear. But the reality of birth and death remains, and no amount of modern science can unravel the mysteries of these two 'eternities' between which is poised the flickering moment of earthly life.[12]

It is these two 'infinities' which determine the character and meaning of the finitude that stands between them. With respect to these two 'infinities' the situation of man has not changed at all even if the destruction of the medieval cosmologies has destroyed for most men the metaphysical doctrine of the states of being that the medieval cosmology symbolized so beautifully. Man is still a finite being with an intelligence made to understand the Infinite and the Absolute and not the indefinite and the relative, whose total grasp lies forever beyond the ken of any human science. With respect to the Absolute and all the states of being which comprise the Universe, man is what he has always been and always will be, an image of the Absolute in the relative, cast into the stream of becoming in order to return this becoming itself to Being. Today there is so much talk of change that men are hypnotized by their own words and forget that just beneath the surface of these ever-moving waves lies the immutable and permanent sea of man's real nature. The situation of this permanent nature which man carries within himself wherever he goes versus the Real in its metaphysical sense has never altered nor can it ever do so. The ontological situation of man in the total scheme of things is forever the same, it is, more than all the other aspects of man's position in the cosmos, as studied in cosmology and the sciences of nature, permanence amidst apparent change.

[12] 'Modern science, which is rationalist as to its subject and materialist as to its object, can describe our situation physically and approximately, but it can tell us nothing about our extra-spatial situation in the total and real Universe.' F. Schuon, *Light on the Ancient Worlds*, trans. by Lord Northbourne, London, 1965, p. 111.

PART II

VII

Seventh-century Sufism and the School of Ibn 'Arabî

The life cycle of a religious tradition is such that in certain of its later phases there is a kind of return to the original golden age when the spiritual forces were most intense and the tradition closest to its celestial source. Such a phase can be discerned in Islamic history during the seventh/thirteenth century, which was witness to a remarkably intense spiritual life reminiscent of the prophetic age itself. It is enough to ponder over the sublime peaks of Sufism of this period, such as Ibn 'Arabî, Ṣadr al-Dîn al-Qunyawî, Jalâl al-Dîn Rûmî and Najm al-Dîn Kubrâ and the whole Central Asian school, to realize the nature of this amazing chapter in the history of Islam and particularly of Sufism. Among the most important features of this period was the establishment of the school of Ibn 'Arabî which gave a new colour to an important segment of Sufism, uniting many different spiritual strands and serving as a basis for many of its later developments. The spread of the teachings of Ibn 'Arabî in the eastern lands of Islam, with which we are particularly concerned in this essay, is without doubt one of the outstanding spiritual and intellectual events of this era.

In the eastern regions of Islam the teachings of Ibn 'Arabî found a most suitable soil for later growth. It was here that his doctrines not only transformed the language of doctrinal Sufism but also penetrated into theology and theosophy or traditional philosophy (*ḥikmah*). For seven centuries whole generations of sages and saints have commented upon his works and to this day his masterpiece, the *Fuṣûṣ al-hikam* or *Bezels of Wisdom*[1], is taught in traditional religious circles as well as in the gatherings of the Sufis and gnostics.[2]

The spread of the teachings of Ibn 'Arabî in these eastern lands

[1] It is unfortunate that as yet there is no completely satisfactory translation of this work in English although there is an excellent translation of its basic passages with illuminating notes in French by T. Burckhardt under the title *La sagesse des prophètes*, Paris, 1955.

[2] See S. H. Nasr, *Three Muslim Sages*, pp. 118 ff. Also H. Corbin, *Creative Imagination in the Sûfism of Ibn 'Arabî*, translated by R. Manheim, London, 1969, chapter I.

and particularly in Persia[3], can best be studied by dividing those who were influenced by him into several distinct categories. There are first of all the well-known Sufis themselves, most of them also masters of the Persian language, in whom elements of the teaching of Muḥyî al-Dîn can be seen in various forms. The greatest Sufi poet of the Persian language, Jalâl al-Dîn Rûmî, who was also immensely influential in the Turkish-speaking world as well as in the Indo-Pakistani subcontinent, is already connected to Ibn 'Arabî through Ṣadr al-Dîn al-Qunyawî who was the disciple of the latter and friend and close associate of the former. Some have called the *Mathnawî* the *Futûḥât* in Persian verse. There is no doubt that there are domains in which there is a close association between these two towering masters of Islamic gnosis. But it must also be remembered that Rûmî represents yet another facet and form of Sufism that is complementary to the approach and particular form of the Sufism of Ibn 'Arabî and not simply its derivative.

After Rûmî other well-known Sufi authors like 'Azîz Nasafî and Sa'd al-Dîn Ḥamûyah, although belonging to the Central Asian school of Najm al-Dîn Kubrâ, likewise display their profound debt to the doctrinal expositions of the Shaykh al-Akbar. Even 'Alâ' al-Dawlah Simnânî, who criticized some of Ibn 'Arabî's formulations, was influenced by him.[4]

Likewise, amid the outstanding Sufi poets of this period, while some like Ḥâfiz and Sa'dî followed the classical imagery and language of Sanâ'î, 'Aṭṭâr and Rûmî or added new dimensions within the same framework while using a symbolic language of similar form, others turned to the teachings of Ibn 'Arabî which they expounded in exquisite Persian poetry or prose. The *Lama'ât* of Fakhr al-Dîn 'Arâqî, a disciple of Ṣadr al-Dîn al-Qunyawî, especially as commented by Jâmî in his *Ashi''at al-lama'ât*, is a perfect example, as are also the poems of Awḥad al-Dîn Kirmânî and the *Gulshan-i râz* (*The*

[3] This distinction needs to be made because a great deal of Sufi writing in India is also in the Persian language, especially that which concerns the debate of this period about Ibn 'Arabî's *waḥdat al-wujûd* and Simnânî's *waḥdat al-shuhûd.* The questions discussed in these debates became later the point of controversy in the writings of Shaykh Aḥmad Sirhindî and others.

[4] Concerning these important figures of Sufism see the many studies of H. Corbin especially those that have appeared in the *Eranos-Jahrbuch*; also M. M. Molé's introduction and notes to Nasafî's *Le livre de l'homme parfait*, Tehran-Paris, 1962, and his 'Les Kubrawiya entre sunnisme et chiisme aux VIIIe et IXe siècles de l'hégire', *Revue des Etudes Islamiques*, vol. 29, 1961 pp. 61–142. A brief account of the influence of Ibn 'Arabî in the East is given by M. Molé in his *Les mystiques musulmans*, Paris, 1965, pp. 100 ff.

Secret Rose Garden) of Maḥmûd Shabistarî. This work contains the synopsis of all Sufi doctrine as expounded by Muḥyî al-Dîn, expressed in verses of celestial beauty that have become the common heritage of all Persian-speaking people and are also very well known in Pakistan and among the Muslims of India. Likewise, the best-known commentator upon the *Gulshan-i râz*, Shaykh Muḥammad Lâhîjî, a founder of the Nûrbakhshî Sufi order, was himself deeply influenced by al-Shaykh al-Akbar, as Ibn 'Arabī is known in the East.

Another great master of Sufism in Persia, Shâh Ni'matullâh Walî, the founder of the Ni'matullâhî order, which is the most widespread order in Persia today with branches in Pakistan and other Muslim lands, rendered the *Fuṣûṣ* into Persian. He also translated the verses of the *Fuṣûṣ* into Persian poetry and commented upon them. Shâh Ni'matullâh confesses openly to his affiliation with Ibn 'Arabî in these verses:

> The words of the *Fuṣûṣ* became set in our heart like a jewel in its station.
> It reached him from the Prophet of God and from his (Ibn 'Arabî's) spirit became attached to us.[5]

No clearer indication is needed to demonstrate the profound connection between Ibn 'Arabî and the most influential Sufi master in the later history of Persia.

To the same type of Sufi poets and masters belongs the great poet 'Abd al-Raḥmân Jâmî, who did much to spread the teachings of Ibn 'Arabî.[6] Through commentaries upon the works of the Shaykh al-Akbar, the composition of original works based on his doctrinal teachings and his own independent poetry and prose compositions, he exerted an immense influence upon his contemporaries and later generations of Persian-speaking Sufis. His example has been followed by many a later poet such as Ṣafâ-yi Iṣfahânî, an outstanding Sufi poet of only two generations ago who was deeply versed in the *Fuṣûṣ* and the writings of Ṣadr al-Dîn al-Qunyawî and who also composed some of the finest Persian Sufi poetry of the last century.

A second category of those influenced by Ibn 'Arabî are the Shi'ite theologians who, by incorporating the teachings of Ibn 'Arabî into

[5] کلمات فصوص در دل ما   چون نگین درا مقام خود بنشست
از رسول خدا رسید باو   بازاز روح او بماپیوست

Risâlah-i abyât-i fuṣûṣ al-ḥikam in the collection *Riḍwân ma'ârif al-ilâhiyyah*, Tehran, cited in Ḥamîd Farzâm, 'Relation de Hafiz et Chah Vali' (in Persian), *Revue de la Faculté des Lettres d'Ispahan*, 1345 (1966) No. 2–3, p. 2.

[6] See Muḥammad Ismâ'îl Muballigh, *Jâmî wa Ibn 'Arabî*, Kabul, 1343 (1964).

the structure of Twelve-Imâm Shi'ism, prepared the ground for the intellectual synthesis of the Safavid period when Persia became predominantly Shi'ite. The whole relation between the doctrines of Ibn 'Arabî and the Shi'ite gnosis into which it became so readily integrated bears close investigation.[7] Soon after the propagation of his teachings, Ibn 'Arabî gained followers among Shi'ite theologians and gnostics such as Sayyid Ḥaydar Âmulî, who even wrote a commentary upon the *Fuṣûṣ*,[8] Ibn Turkah, whose *Tamhîd al-qawâ'id* is an introduction to the *Fuṣûṣ* and who wrote an important commentary upon this work, and Ibn Abî Jumhûr, who in his *Kitâb al-mujlî* reflects many of the Shaykh al-Akbar's doctrines.

One must also remember the influence of Ibn 'Arabî on Ismâ'îlî authors, many of whom wrote in Persian although their later home was to become India. To this day the most widely read commentary upon the Holy Quran among Ismâ'îlîs is that attributed to Ibn 'Arabî, who is curiously enough considered by many Ismâ'îlîs to have been one of them. The whole group of Ismâ'îlî authors writing in Persian in the seventh/thirteenth and eighth/fourteenth centuries and until Isma'ilism went underground in Persia comprise one of the most noteworthy and curious extensions of the teachings of Ibn 'Arabî within the world of Islam.

With the advent of the Safavids a renaissance took place in Islamic philosophy in Persia, the highlight of which is the appearance of Ṣadr al-Dîn Shîrâzî or Mullâ Ṣadrâ. Combining the tenets of Peripatetic philosophy and *ishrâqî* or Illuminationist doctrines and the gnosis (*'irfân*) of Ibn 'Arabî, this great sage was able to create a new intellectual perspective and a school that survives in Persia to this day.[9] Mullâ Ṣadrâ was deeply impregnated with the teachings of Ibn 'Arabî; his chief work, the *Asfâr*, is replete with quotations from the *Fuṣûṣ* and reflects, especially in doctrines concerned with the

[7] Some attention has been paid to this question by Corbin from the particular point of view of Shi'ite esotericism. A more general investigation, taking into account the fact that Ibn 'Arabî was confessionally a Sunnî yet at the same time became so dear to the hearts of the Shi'ite gnostics, needs to be made in order to clarify the position of Ibn 'Arabî's doctrines in relation to the whole structure of Shi'ism and of Islam in general.

[8] The works of Sayyid Ḥaydar Âmulî are currently being studied and investigated by H. Corbin. See the latter's 'Sayyed Ḥaydar Âmolî (VIIIe/XIVe siècle) théologien shî'ite du soufisme,' *Melanges Henri Massé*, Tehran, 1963, pp. 72–101 and especially his introduction to Âmulî's *Jâmi' al-asrâr*, edited by him and O. Yahya as *La philosophie shi'ite*, Tehran-Paris, 1969.

[9] Concerning Mullâ Ṣadrâ see H. Corbin (ed.), *Le livre des pénétrations métaphysiques* of Ṣadr al-Dîn Shîrâzî, Tehran-Paris, 1964, introduction; also, S. H. Nasr, *Islamic Studies*, part III.

faculties of the soul and eschatology, the teachings of Shaykh al-Akbar.

It would not be too much to say that in most circles and especially in the official religious schools it has been mainly through the works of Mullâ Ṣadrâ and his disciples like Mullâ Na'îmâ Ṭâliqânî, Mullâ 'Alî Nûrî, Ḥâjjî Mullâ Hâdî Sabziwârî, Mullâ 'Alî Zunûzî and Âqâ Muḥammad Riḍâ Qumsha'î that Ibn 'Arabî's doctrines have come to be known in Persia during the past few centuries. The role of Ibn 'Arabî in the creation of this important school of *ḥikmah* is yet another and indeed one of the most significant aspects of his influence in the eastern regions of the Islamic world.

Finally, mention must be made of the direct commentators and interpreters of Ibn 'Arabî, who are his lineal heirs and the continuators of his teachings. Among these figures the most important as far as the eastern lands of Islam in general and Persia in particular are concerned is Ṣadr al-Dîn al-Qunyawî, the disciple and step-son of Ibn 'Arabî from Qunya, through whom the teachings of the master reached these lands.[10]

Himself a great Sufi master, al-Qunyawî commented upon the works of the Shaykh al-Akbar besides writing original works of his own like *Nuṣûṣ*, *Fukûk* and *Miftâḥ al-ghayb*, which along with its commentary *Misbâḥ al-uns* by Ḥamzah Fanârî is considered in Persia as the most advanced text on Sufi metaphysics.[11] In Persia the commentary of Qunyawî on the *Fuṣûṣ* is the most highly esteemed of all the commentaries along with those of 'Abd al-Razzâq Kâshânî and Dâ'ûd Qayṣarî.

Although many other commentaries have been written on the *Fuṣûṣ* in both Arabic and Persian and also Turkish, those of 'Alî Hamadânî, 'Alâ' al-Dawlah Simnânî and the famous one by Jâmî being especially important from the point of view of the Persian language, these are considered as standing below the three above-mentioned commentaries and in many cases, such as that of Jâmî, to have been derived from them. Kâshânî and Qayṣarî are, in fact, after Qunyawî the most important propagators of the doctrines of Ibn 'Arabî in the East, Qayṣarî through his outstanding commentary

[10] To understand the extent of Ibn 'Arabî's influence in Persia it is enough to realize that, according to what has been discovered by Othman Yahya, of the nearly 150 known commentaries upon the *Fuṣûṣ* about 120 are by Persians and other peoples of this region. Concerning these commentaries see O. Yahya, *La classification de l'oeuvre d'Ibn 'Arabî*, vol. I, Damascus, 1964, pp. 247 ff.

[11] It is indeed curious that very few studies have been made of this outstanding master of Sufism whose influence has been so enormous.

which begins with an independent introduction containing a complete cycle of Sufi metaphysics,[12] and Kâshânî through his commentary as well as his *Ta'wîl al-qur'ân* and many other well-known works. As for other celebrated commentaries of the *Fuṣûṣ*, such as those of Bâlî Afandî and Nablusî as well as the many works of Sha'rânî that elucidate the teachings of Ibn 'Arabî, though these have become famous in the Arab world, they became known only to a few in the East and have never enjoyed the same fame and popularity in Persia, Pakistan and India as those mentioned above.

The tradition of teaching and commenting upon the *Fuṣûṣ* and other works of Ibn 'Arabî has continued during the Ottoman, Safavid and Moghul periods and even afterwards to the present day, although its detailed history is by no means clear. In Persia there appeared masters like Mullâ Ḥasan Lunbânî, Mîr Sayyid Ḥasan Ṭâliqânî Mullâ Muḥammad Ja'far Âbâdihî, Sayyid Raḍî Mâzandarânî and Mîrzâ Hâshim Rashtî some of whose disciples are still alive, who span the period from the eleventh/seventeenth and twelfth/eighteenth centuries to the present day. Similarly many Arab, Turkish and Indo-Pakistani commentators appeared, many of whose works have not as yet been fully studied.[13] There have also been commentaries made in China, Malaya and Indonesia following the better-known commentaries of the Persian and Arabic worlds. Most of the masters who have commented upon the *Fuṣûṣ* have also taught it in circles in the *madrasah* or at private gatherings at home and some have written commentaries upon the works of Ṣadr al-Dîn al-Qunyawî as well. More than that, they have transmitted an oral metaphysical tradition, which has been rejuvenated in each generation by these and other masters through their own fresh vision of spiritual realities made possible by the practice of spiritual methods belonging to the esotericism of Islam.

All these groups briefly mentioned here represent different aspects of the extensions of the teachings of Ibn 'Arabî in Persia and other eastern lands of the Islamic world. The doctrines of the Shaykh al-Akbar were to spread to all the lands of Islam and to bear spiritual fruits of varying taste and perfume. They became a major component

[12] See Sayyid Jalâl al-Dîn Âshtiyânî, *Sharḥ-i muqaddimah-i Qayṣarî bar Fuṣûṣ al-ḥikam*, prefaces by H. Corbin and S. H. Nasr, Mashhad, 1966, which contains an elaborate Persian commentary upon the introduction of Qayṣarî. S. J. Âshtiyânî's introduction to the work includes in addition a learned discussion of the commentary of Qayṣarî itself as well as other commentaries.

[13] S. J. Âshtiyânî is preparing a large two-volume commentary upon the *Fuṣûṣ* itself, in the introduction of which he has made a careful study of all the important commentaries, giving the particular characteristics of each.

in that enormous corpus of Sufi metaphysics and gnosis that has cast its light in numerous shades and colours upon all the lands that have come to constitute the *dâr al-islâm*. This school of Sufism became a permanent element in the intellectual life of this world, whereof strands can be found in the very texture of its intellectual and spiritual life to this day.

VIII

Shi'ism and Sufism: their Relationship in Essence and in History

One of the most difficult questions touching the manifestation of Sufism in Islamic history is its relation with Shi'ism. In discussing this intricate and somewhat complex relationship, in principle and essence or in the light of its metahistorical reality as well as in time and history, we need hardly concern ourselves with the too-often repeated criticism made by certain orientalists who would doubt the Islamic and Quranic character of both Shi'ism and Sufism. Basing themselves on an *a priori* assumption that Islam is not a revelation and that even if it ranks as a religion, it is only an elementary 'religion of the sword' intended for a simple desert people, these would-be critics brush aside as un-Islamic all that speaks of gnosis (*'irfân*) and esotericism, pointing to the lack of historical texts in the early period as proof of their thesis—as if the non-existent in itself could disprove the existence of something which may have been there without leaving a written trace for us to dissect and analyse today. The reality of Shi'ism and Sufism as integral aspects of the Islamic revelation is too dazzlingly clear to be ignored or explained away on the basis of a tendentious historical argument. The fruit is there to prove that the tree has its roots in a soil that nourishes it; and the spiritual fruit can only be borne by a tree whose roots are sunk in a revealed truth. To deny this most evident of truths would be as if one were to doubt the Christian sanctity of St Francis of Assisi because the historical records of the first years of the Apostolic succession are not documented to fit academic standards. What the presence of St Francis proves is in reality the opposite fact, namely, that the Apostolic succession must be real even if no historical records are at hand. The same holds true *mutatis mutandis* for Shi'ism and Sufism. In this essay we will in any case begin by taking for granted the Islamic character of Shi'ism and Sufism as covered previously in this book and elsewhere and upon this basis we can delve into their relationship.[1] In fact Shi'ism and

[1] The author has dealt with the Islamic origin of Shi'ism and Sufism in *Three Muslim Sages*, pp. 83–90; and *Ideals and Realities of Islam*, chapter V; see also H. Corbin (with the collaboration of S. H. Nasr and O. Yahya), *Histoire de la*

Sufism are both, in different ways and on different levels, intrinsic aspects of Islamic orthodoxy, this term being taken not merely in its theological sense but more especially in its universal sense as tradition and universal truth contained within a revealed form.

The relationship between Shi'ism and Sufism is complicated by the fact that in discussing these two spiritual and religious realities we are not dealing with the same level or dimension of Islam in both cases. As already mentioned, Islam has both an exoteric (*ẓâhir*) and an esoteric (*bâṭin*) dimension, which along with all their inner divisions represent the 'vertical' structure of the revelation. But it is also divided into Sunnism and Shi'ism, which one might say represent its 'horizontal' structure.[2] Were this the only aspect of the above relationship it would be relatively simple to explain. But as a matter of fact the esoteric dimension of Islam, which in the Sunni climate is almost totally connected with Sufism, in one way or another colours the whole structure of Shi'ism in both its esoteric and even its exoteric aspect. One can say that Islamic esotericism or gnosis crystallized into the form of Sufism in the Sunni world while it poured into the whole structure of Shi'ism especially during its early period.[3] From the Sunni point of view Sufism presents similarities to Shi'ism and has even assimilated aspects thereof. No less an authority than Ibn Khaldûn writes: 'The Sufis thus became saturated with Shi'ah theories. (Shi'ah) theories entered so deeply into their religious ideas that they based their own practice of using a cloak (*khirqah*) on the

philosophie islamique, vol. 1, Paris, 1964, part one. Concerning the Islamic origin of Sufism see Abû Bakr Sirâj ed-Dîn, 'The Origins of Sufism', *Islamic Quarterly*, April, 1956, vol. III, pp. 53-64; F. Schuon, *Understanding Islam*, chapter IV; and R. Guénon, 'L'Esotérisme islamique', in *L'Islam et l'Occident*, Paris, 1947, pp. 153–9.

Besides Corbin, some of the earlier Western scholars have also emphasized the close connection between Shi'ism and Sufism. See T. Andrae, *Die Person Muhammads im Leben und Glauben seiner Gemeinde*, Stockholm, 1918, where however in contrast to Corbin everything of an esoteric character in Islam is relegated to Hellenistic and Christian sources.

[2] Concerning these relationships see Nasr, *Ideals and Realities of Islam*, chapter VI.

[3] 'On ne peut plus, en tout rigeur, faire de "soufisme" et de mystique musulmane, deux termes interchangeables depuis que l'on sait, en particulier grâce aux travaux de H. Corbin, qu'il existe une mystique musulmane—la gnose ismaélienne et imâmite notamment—qui ne se reconnâit pas "soufique". Toutefois, ce qui est dit ici du *taṣawwuf* à ses débuts vaut également pour cette mystique, ou gnose non soufique, laquelle a aussi sa source dans les enseignements du Prophète et de certains compagnons, dont surtout 'Alî.' J. L. Michon, *Le soufi marocain Aḥmed ibn Ajîba et son mi'râj* (Thése de doctorat, Faculté des Lettres, Université de Paris, 1960, p. 2, n. 1.)

fact that 'Alî clothed al-Ḥasan al-Baṣrî in such a cloak and caused him to agree solemnly that he would adhere to the mystic path. (The tradition thus inaugurated by 'Alî) was continued according to the Sufis, through al-Junayd, one of the Sufi *shaykhs*.'[4] From the Shi'ite point of view Shi'ism is the origin of what later came to be known as Sufism. But here by Shi'ism is meant the esoteric instructions of the Prophet, the *asrâr* which many Shi'ite authors have identified with the Shi'ite 'concealment', *taqiyyah*.

Each of these two points of view presents an aspect of the same reality but seen within two worlds that are contained in the bosom of the total orthodoxy of Islam. That reality is Islamic esotericism or gnosis. If we take Sufism and Shi'ism in their historical manifestation in later periods, then neither Shi'ism nor Sunnism, nor Sufism within the Sunni world, derive from one another. They all derive their authority from the Prophet and the source of the Islamic revelation. But if we mean by Shi'ism Islamic esotericism as such, then it is of course inseparable from Sufism. For example, the Shi'ite Imâms play a fundamental role in Sufism, but as representatives of Islamic esotericism, not as specifically Shi'ite Imâms according to the later organization of the Shi'ite faith. In fact there is a tendency among both later Muslim historians and modern scholars to read back into the first two centuries the clear distinctions that were established only later.[5] It is true that one can discern 'Shi'ite' elements even during the life-time of the Prophet and that Shi'ism and Sunnism have their roots in the very origin of the Islamic revelation, placed there providentially to accommodate different psychological and ethnic types. But the hard-and-fast divisions of later centuries are not discernible in the earlier period. There were Sunni elements with definite Shi'ite tendencies,[6] and there were Shi'ite contacts with

[4] Ibn Khaldûn, *Muqaddimah*, trans. by F. Rosenthal, vol. II, New York, 1958, p. 187. Ibn Khaldûn continues, 'The fact that (the Sufis) restrict (precedence in mysticism) to 'Alî smells strongly of pro-Shî'ah sentiment. This and other aforementioned Sufi ideas show that the Sufis have adopted pro-Shî'ah sentiments and have become enmeshed in them.' *Ibid.*, p. 187.

On this question see also the extensive and well-documented work of Kâmil al-Shîbî, *al-Ṣilah bayn al-taṣawwuf wa'l-tashayyu'*, 2 vols., Baghdad, 1963-64.

[5] This anachronistic practice is criticized by John B. Taylor in his 'Ja'far al-Ṣâdiq, Spiritual Forebear of the Sufis', *Islamic Culture*, vol. XL, no. 2, April 1966, pp. 97 ff.

[6] 'So many-sided is this Sunni sentiment—in *ḥadîths*, in the Sufi orders, in guilds, in popular tales—that not only in its support of the original 'Alid claims but in its whole piety Sunni Islam can be called half Shî'ite'. M. G. S. Hodgson, 'How did the early Shî'a become Sectarian?" *Journal of the American Oriental Society*, vol. 75, 1955, p. 4. See also J. B. Taylor, 'An Approach to the Emergence of

Sunni elements both intellectually and socially. In certain cases in fact it is difficult to judge as to whether a particular author was Shi'ite or Sunni especially before the fourth/tenth century, although even in this period Shi'ite and Sunni religious and spiritual life each possessed its own particular perfume and colour.

In this less crystallized and more fluid environment, those elements of Islamic esotericism which from the Shi'ite point of view are considered as particularly Shi'ite, appear as representing Islamic esotericism as such in the Sunni world. No better instance of this can be found than the person of 'Alî ibn Abî Ṭâlib. Shi'ism may be called the 'Islam of 'Alî', who in Shi'ism is both the 'spiritual' and 'temporal' authority after the Prophet. In Sunnism also nearly all Sufi orders reach back to him and he is the spiritual authority *par excellence* after the Prophet.[7] The famous *ḥadîth* 'I am the city of knowledge and 'Alî is its gate', which is a direct reference to the role of 'Alî in Islamic esotericism, is accepted by Shi'ah and Sunni alike, but the 'spiritual vicegerency' (*khilâfah rûḥâniyyah*) of 'Alî appears to Sufism within the Sunni world not as something specifically Shi'ite but as being directly connected with Islamic esotericism in itself.

Yet the case of 'Alî, the reverence in which he is held by Shi'ites and Sufis alike, shows how intimately Shi'ism and Sufism are connected together. Sufism does not possess a *Sharî'ah*; it is only a spiritual way (*Ṭarîqah*) attached to a particular Shari'ite rite such as the *Mâlikî* or *Shâfi'î*. Shi'ism possesses both a *Sharî'ah* and a *Ṭarîqah*. In its purely spiritual or *Ṭarîqah* aspect it is in many instances identical with Sufism as it exists in the Sunni world, and certain Sufi orders such as the Ni'matullâhî have existed in both the Shi'ite and Sunni worlds. But in addition Shi'ism possesses even in its Shari'ite and theological aspects certain esoteric elements which make it akin to Sufism. In fact one could say that Shi'ism, even in its outward aspect, is oriented toward the spiritual stations (*maqâmât-i 'irfânî*) of the Prophet and the Imâms, which are also the goal of the spiritual life in Sufism.

A few examples in the vast and intricate relationship between Shi'ism and Sufism may make more clear some of the points discussed so far. In Islam in general, and Sufism in particular, a saint is called a

Heterodoxy in Medieval Islam', *Religious Studies*, vol. II, April 1967, p. 202, where the words of Hodgson are also quoted.

In certain areas of the Islamic world, particularly in the Indo-Pakistani subcontinent, one meets among Sufis certain groups as devoted to the Shi'ite Imâms, especially 'Alî and Ḥusayn, as any Shî'ite could be, yet completely Sunni in their practice of the law (*madhhab*).

[7] See F. Schuon, 'De la tradition monothéiste', *Etudes Traditionelles*, 1933, p. 257.

walî (abbreviation of *walîallâh* or friend of God) and sanctity is called *wilâyah.* As already mentioned in Shi'ism the whole function of the Imâm is associated with the power and function of what in Persian is called *walâyat*, which comes from the same root as *wilâyah* and is closely connected with it.[8] Some have even identified the two. In any case according to Shi'ism, in addition to the power of prophecy in the sense of bringing a divine law (*nubuwwah* and *risâlah*), the Prophet of Islam, like other great prophets before him, had the power of spiritual guidance and initiation (*walâyah*) which he transmitted to Fâṭimah and 'Alî and through them to all the Imâms. Since the Imâm is always alive, this function and power is also always present in this world and able to guide men to the spiritual life. The 'cycle of initiation' (*dâ'irat al-walâyah*) which follows the 'cycle of prophecy' (*dâ'irat al-nubuwwah*) is therefore one that continues to this day and guarantees the ever-living presence of an esoteric way in Islam.[9]

The same meaning pertains to *wilâyah* in the sense that it too concerns the ever-living spiritual presence in Islam which enables men to practise the spiritual life and to reach a state of sanctity. That is why many Sufis since the time of Ḥakîm al-Tirmidhî have devoted so much attention to this cardinal aspect of Sufism.[10] There is to be sure a difference between Shi'ism and Sufism on how and through whom this power and function operates as well as who is considered as its 'seal'.[11] But the similarity between the Shi'ah and the Sufis concerning this doctrine is most startling and results directly from the fact that both are connected in the manner mentioned above with Islamic esotericism as such, which is none other than *wilâyah* or *walâyah* as used in the technical sense in both Shi'ite and Sufi sources.

Among the practices of the Sufis there is one that is closely associated in its symbolic meaning with *wilâyah* and in its origin with the Shi'ite

[8] See H. Corbin, 'L'Imâm caché et la rénovation de l'homme en théologie shî'ite', *Eranos-Jahrbuch*, 1960, pp. 87 ff.

[9] On the 'cycles of initiation and prophecy', see S. H. Nasr, *Ideals and Realities of Islam*, pp. 87 and 161; and H. Corbin, *op. cit.*

[10] Ḥâkim al-Tirmidhî devoted a major work to this question entitled *Khatm al-awliyâ'* which has been recently edited by O. Yahya and which had much influence upon Ibn 'Arabî and later Sufis.

[11] Ibn 'Arabî and following him Dâ'ûd al-Qayṣarî consider Christ as the universal 'seal of sanctity', and Ibn 'Arabî refers indirectly to himself as the 'particular seal of sanctity' whereas most Shi'ite authors believe these titles belong to 'Alî and the Mahdî respectively. In this delicate question the distinction between the 'universal seal of sanctity' and the 'particular or Muḥammadan seal of sanctity' must be kept especially in mind. In any case this is a point of contention between Ibn 'Arabî and even his most ardent Shi'ite followers such as Sayyid Ḥaydar Âmulî.

walâyah. It is the practice of wearing a cloak and handing it from the master to the disciple as a symbol of the transmission of a spiritual teaching and the particular grace associated with the act of initiation. Each state of being is like a cloak or veil that 'covers' the state above, for symbolically the 'above' is associated with the 'inward'. The Sufi cloak symbolizes the transmission of spiritual power which enables the disciple or *murîd* to penetrate beyond his everyday state of consciousness. By virtue of being presented with this cloak or veil in its symbolic sense he is able to cast aside the inner veil that separates him from the Divine.

The practice of wearing and transmitting the cloak and the meaning of this act are closely associated with Shiʿism, as affirmed by Ibn Khaldûn in the quotation cited above. According to the famous *Ḥadîth-i kisâ'* (the tradition of the garment) the Prophet called his daughter Fâṭimah along with ʿAlî, Ḥasan and Ḥusayn and placed a cloak upon them in such a manner that it covered them.[12] The cloak symbolizes the transmission of the universal *walâyah* of the Prophet in the form of the partial *walâyah* (*walâyat-i fâṭimiyyah*) to Fâṭimah and through her to the Imâms who were her descendents. There is a direct reference to the esoteric symbolism of the cloak in a well-known Shiʿite *ḥadîth* which because of its significance and beauty is quoted fully here:

'It has been accounted of the Prophet—upon him and his family be peace—that he said: "When I was taken on the nocturnal ascension to heaven and I entered paradise, I saw in the middle of it a palace made of red rubies. Gabriel opened the door for me and I entered it. I saw in it a house made of white pearls. I entered the house and saw in the middle of it a box made of light and locked with a lock made of light. I said, 'Oh, Gabriel, what is this box and what is in it?' Gabriel said, 'Oh Friend of God (*Ḥabîballâh*), in it is the secret of God (*sirrallâh*) which God does not reveal to anyone except to him whom He loves.' I said, 'Open its door for me'. He said, 'I am a slave who follows the divine command. Ask thy Lord until He grants permission to open it.' I therefore asked for the permission of God. A voice came from the Divine Throne saying, 'Oh Gabriel open its door', and he opened it. In it I saw spiritual poverty (*faqr*) and a cloak (*muraqqaʿ*). I said, 'What is this *faqr* and *muraqqaʿ*?' The voice from heaven said, 'Oh Muḥammad, there are two things which I have chosen for thee and thy people (*ummah*) from the moment I created the two of you. These two things I do not give to anyone save those whom I love, and I have

[12] This *ḥadîth* appears in many different forms in Shîʿite sources such as the *Ghâyat al-marâm*, Tehran, 1272, pp. 287 ff.

created nothing dearer than these.'" Then the Holy Prophet said, "God—Exalted be His Name—selected *faqr* and the *muraqqa'* for me and these two are the dearest things to Him." The Prophet directed his attention toward God and when he returned from the nocturnal ascent (*mi'râj*) he made 'Alî wear the cloak with the permission of God and by His command. 'Alî wore it and sewed patches on it until he said, "I have sewn so many patches on this cloak that I am embarrassed before the sewer." 'Alî made his son Ḥasan to wear it after him and then Ḥusayn and then the descendants of Ḥusayn one after another until the Mahdî. The cloak rests with him now.'[13]

Ibn Abî Jumhûr as well as the later Shi'ite commentators upon this *ḥadîth* add that the cloak worn and transmitted by the Sufis is not the same cloak cited in the *ḥadîth*. Rather, what the Sufis seek to do is to emulate the conditions for wearing the cloak as the Prophet wore it and through this act to become aware to the extent of their capability of the divine mysteries (*asrâr*) which the cloak symbolises.

The whole question of *walâyah* and the cloak that symbolises it makes clear the most important common element between Sufism and Shi'ism, which is the presence of a hidden form of knowledge and instruction. The use of the method of *ta'wîl* or spiritual hermeneutics in the understanding of the Holy Quran as well as of the 'cosmic text', and belief in grades of meaning within the revelation—both of which are common to Sufism and Shi'ism—result from the presence of this esoteric form of knowledge. The presence of *walâyat* guarantees for Shi'ism and Sufism alike a gnostic and esoteric character, of which the doctrine and the characteristic manner of instruction present in both are natural expressions.

Closely associated with *walâyah* is the concept of the Imâm in Shi'ism, for the Imâm is he who possesses the power and function of *walâyat*. The role of the Imâm is central to Shi'ism, but we cannot deal here with all its ramifications.[14] But from the spiritual point of

[13] Ibn Abî Jumhûr, *Kitâb al-mujlî*, Tehran, 1329, p. 379. This *ḥadîth* has been mentioned with slight variations by many Shî'ite gnostics and Sufis. See for example, Muḥammad 'Alî Sabziwârî, *Tuḥfat al-'abbâsiyyah*, Shiraz, 1326, pp. 93–4. Many other Shi'ite and also Sunni authors like Ibn Abi'l-Ḥadîd, Maytham al-Baḥrânî and Sayyid Ḥaydar Âmulî have referred to this *ḥadîth*. See al-Shîbî, *al-Ṣilah bayn al-taṣawwuf wa'l-tashayyu'*, vol. II, p. 117.

[14] On the role of the Imâm in Shi'ite spirituality see the many works of H. Corbin in the *Eranos-Jahrbuch* especially 'L'Imâm caché et la rénovation de l'homme en théologie Shî'ite', and 'Pour une morphologie de la spiritualité Shî'ite', *Eranos-Jahrbuch*, vol. XXIX, 1961.

view it is important to point to his function as the spiritual guide, a function that closely resembles that of the Sufi master. The Shiʿite seeks to encounter his Imâm, who is none other than the inner spiritual guide—so that some Shiʿite Sufis speak of the Imâm of each person's being (*imâm wujûdika*). If one leaves aside the Shariʿite and also cosmic functions of the Imâm, his initiatory function and role as spiritual guide is similar to that of the Sufi master.

In fact just as in Sufism each master is in contact with the pole (*Quṭb*) of his age, in Shiʿism all spiritual functions in every age are inwardly connected with the Imâm. The idea of the Imâm as the pole of the Universe and the concept of the *Quṭb* in Sufism are nearly identical, as asserted so clearly by Sayyid Ḥaydar Âmulî when he says, 'The *Quṭb* and the Imâm are two expressions possessing the same meaning and referring to the same person.'[15] The doctrine of the universal or perfect man (*al-insân al-kâmil*)[16] as expounded by Ibn ʿArabî is very similar to the Shiʿite doctrine of the *Quṭb* and the Imâm, as is the doctrine of the Mahdî developed by later Sufi masters. All these doctrines refer essentially and ultimately to the same esoteric reality, the *ḥaqîqat al-muḥammadiyyah*, as present in both Shiʿism and Sufism. And in this case as far as the formulation of this doctrine is concerned there may have been direct Shiʿite influences upon later Sufi formulations.[17]

Another doctrine that is shared in somewhat different forms by Shiʿites and Sufis is that of the 'Muḥammadan light' (*al-nûr al-muḥammadî*) and the initiatic chain (*silsilah*). Shiʿism believes that there is a 'Primordial Light' passed from one prophet to another and after the Prophet of Islam to the Imâms. This light protects the prophets and Imâms from sin, making them inerrant (*maʿṣûm*), and bestows upon them the knowledge of divine mysteries. In order to gain this knowledge man must become attached to this light through the Imâm who, following the Prophet, acts as man's intermediary with God in the quest for divine knowledge. In the same way, in Sufism, in order to gain access to the methods which alone make spiritual realisation possible, man must become attached to an initiatory chain or *silsilah* which goes back to the Prophet and through which a

FT.?

[15] Sayyid Ḥaydar Âmulî, *La philosophie shîʿite*, p. 223; and also quoted by Kâmil al-Shîbî, *al-Fikr al-shîʿî wa'l-nazaʿât al-ṣûfiyyah*, Baghdad, 1966, p. 123.

[16] Concerning the Sufi doctrine of the universal man see the translation of al-Jîlî's *al-Insân al-kâmil* by T. Burckhardt as *De l'homme universel*, Lyons, 1953; also R. Guénon, *Symbolism of the Cross*, trans. by A. Macnab, London, 1958.

[17] Al-Shîbî in his *al-Ṣilah*. . ., vol. II, pp. 52–3, writes that Ibn ʿArabî has made use of Shiʿite sources in formulating his doctrines of the *ḥaqîqat al-muḥammadiyyah*, *waḥdat al-wujûd* and the Mahdî.

barakah flows from the source of revelation to the being of the initiate. The chain is thus based on a continuity of spiritual presence that much resembles the 'Muḥammadan light' of Shi'ism. In fact later Sufis themselves also speak of the 'Muḥammadan light'. In the early period, especially in teachings of Imâm Ja'far al-Ṣâdiq, the Shi'ite doctrine of the 'Muḥammadan light' and the Sufi doctrine of the spiritual chain meet, and as in other cases have their source in the same esoteric teachings of Islam.[18]

Finally, in this comparison between Shi'ite and Sufi doctrines one should mention the spiritual and gnostic stations (*maqâmât-i 'irfânî*). If we turn to a study of the life of the Prophet and the Imâms as, for example, found in the compilation of Majlisî in the *Biḥâr al-anwâr*, we will discover that these accounts are based more than anything else upon the inner spiritual states of the personages concerned. The goal of the religious life in Shi'ism is, in fact, to emulate the life of the Prophet and the Imâms and to reach their inward states. Although for the majority of Shi'ites this remains only a latent possibility, the élite (*khawâṣṣ*) have always been fully aware of it. The spiritual stations of the Prophet and the Imâms leading to union with God can be considered as the final goal toward which Shi'ite piety strives and upon which the whole spiritual structure of Shi'ism is based.

Now in Sufism also, the goal, which is to reach God, cannot be achieved except through the states and stations (*ḥâl* and *maqâm*) which occupy such a prominent position in the classical treatises of Sufism. The Sufi life is also one that is based on the achievement of these states, although the Sufi does not seek these states in themselves but seeks God in His Exalted Essence. Of course in Sufism nearly all the members of an order are conscious of the states and stations whereas in Shi'ism only the élite are aware of them, but this is quite natural inasmuch as Sufism as such is the path for the spiritual élite whereas Shi'ism concerns a whole community, possessing its own exoteric and esoteric division and having its own élite as well as its common believers (*'awâmm*). But in the special significance given to the spiritual stations in the Shi'ite account of the lives of the Prophet and the Imâms, there is a striking similarity with what one finds in Sufism. Here again both refer to the same reality, Islamic esotericism, with the practical and realised aspect of which the spiritual stations are concerned.

Having considered these few instances of the relationship between

[18] On Imâm Ja'far's teaching on this subject as it pertains to both Shi'ism and Sufism see Taylor, 'Ja'far al-Ṣadîq, Spiritual Forebear of the Sufis', pp. 101–2.

Shi'ism and Sufism in principle we must now discuss briefly how the relationship between the two has manifested itself in Islamic history.[19] During the life-time of the Imâms, from the first to the eighth, the contact between the two was most intimate. The writings of the Imâms contain a treasury of Islamic gnosis. The *Nahj al-balâghah* of 'Alî,[20] one of the most neglected works of Islam in modern studies of the Western Islamicists, the *Ṣaḥîfah sajjâdiyyah* of the fourth Imâm, Zayn al-'âbidîn, called the 'Psalms of the Family of the Prophet',[21] and the *Uṣûl al-kâfî* of Kulaynî, containing the sayings of the Imâms, outline a complete exposition of Islamic gnosis and have served in fact as a basis for many later gnostic and Sufi commentaries. Although their technical vocabulary is not in all respects the same as the works of the early Sufis, as shown by Massignon,[22] the doctrines and spiritual expositions contained therein are essentially the same as one finds in the classical Sufi treatises.

During this period of the lifetime of the Imâms there was intimate

[19] This is a very complex question which of necessity can only be treated here in very summary fashion. A fairly extensive survey of this question is found in the two works of al-Shîbî, *al-Ṣilah* . . . and *al-Fikr al-shî'î wa'l-naza'ât al-ṣûfiyyah*, but even these two scholarly works deal mostly with the central lands of Islam leaving out of discussion the Maghrib, much of Central Asia and especially India, where the relation between Shi'ism and Sufism has produced results not found elsewhere, results which should be closely studied.

[20] On the pretext that the *Nahj al-balâghah* is not by 'Alî but comes from the pen of its compiler Sayyid Sharîf Raḍî, many Western orientalists have simply dismissed it as unauthentic. First of all many of the sayings compiled in the *Nahj al-balâghah* exist in texts antedating Raḍî, secondly their style is totally different from the many books that have survived from Raḍî's pen and finally their innate quality is sufficient guarantee of their celestial inspiration. Today there are too many works of purely spiritual character which are brushed aside by simply attaching the name 'pseudo' to them or by doubting their authority with total disregard for the innate value of their content.

A few years ago in a session in which the famous Shi'ite theologian and gnostic, 'Allâmah Sayyid Muḥammad Ḥusayn Ṭabâṭabâ'î, and Professor Henry Corbin were present, Professor Corbin asked the Shi'ite authority as to whether the *Nahj al-balâghah* was the work of 'Alî, the first Imâm. 'Allâmah Ṭabâṭabâ'î answered, 'He who has written the *Nahj al-balâghah* is for us the Imâm even if he lived a century ago.'

In any case it is curious that through completely inadequate historical arguments which do not at all disprove its authenticity, the *Nahj al-balâghah*, a book which is the most revered in Shi'ism after the Quran and prophetic sayings and which has taught so many famous Arab writers such as Kurd 'Alî and Ṭâhâ Ḥusayn how to write eloquent Arabic, has been neglected to this extent.

[21] *Zabûr-i âl-i Muḥammad.*

[22] See especially his *Essai sur les origines du lexique technique de la mystique musulmane*, Paris, 1954, and *Recueil de textes inédits concernant l'histoire de la mystique en pays d'Islam*, Paris, 1929.

contact between the Imâms and some of the greatest of the early Sufis. Ḥasan al-Baṣrî and Uways al-Qaranî were disciples of 'Alî; Ibrâhîm al-Adham, Bishr al-Ḥâfî and Bâyazîd al-Basṭâmî were associated with the circle of Imâm Ja'far al-Ṣâdiq; and Ma'rûf al-Karkhî was a close companion of Imâm Riḍâ. Moreover, the earliest Sufis, before being called by this name, were known as ascetics (*zuhhâd*) and many of them were associated with the Imâms and followed their example in the ascetic life. In Kufa such men as Kumayl, Maytham al-Tammâr, Rashîd al-Ḥajarî, all of whom were among the early Sufis and ascetics, belonged to the entourage of the Imâms. The 'companions of the ledge' (*aṣḥâb al-ṣuffah*) before them, like Salmân, Abû Dharr and 'Ammâr al-Yâsir, are also both poles of early Sufism and the early members of the Shi'ite community.[23]

FT. It was only after the eighth Imâm, 'Alî al-Riḍâ, that the Shi'ite Imâms no longer associated themselves openly with the Sufis. It is not that they spoke against Sufism as some exoteric Shi'ite critics of Sufism have claimed. Rather, because of special conditions prevailing at that time they remained silent in these matters. Imâm Riḍâ thus appears as the last explicit and open link between Sufism and the Shi'ite Imâms. To this day he is in fact considered as the 'Imâm of initiation' and many Persians who seek a spiritual master and initiation into Sufism go to his tomb in Mashhad to pray for his help in finding a master. For this reason also his role in the Shi'ite Sufi orders has been great to this day.

After the Imâms, Shi'ism and Sufism became both distinct in themselves and to a certain extent separated from each other. During this period, in contrast to the life-time of the Imâms, Shi'ism began to have a more active political role while most of the Sufis, at least in the third/ninth and fourth/tenth centuries, shied away from participation in political life and all that possessed a worldly aspect. Yet some of the Sufis like al-Ḥallâj were definitely Shi'ite or of Shi'ite tendency and there are certain relations between Sufism and Shi'ism, particularly in its Ismâ'îlî form, as we see in clear references to Sufism in the *Epistles* of the Brethren of Purity, which if not definitely Ismâ'îlî in origin certainly come from a Shi'ite background and are later closely associated with Isma'ilism.[24] Twelve-Imâm Shi'ism also showed some links with Sufism. Ibn Bâbûyah, the famous Shi'ite theologian, describes the Sufi circle (*ḥalqah*) in which invocation (*dhikr*) is per-

[23] The relationship between the Imâms and the first generations of *zuhhâd* that later became known as Sufis is discussed by 'Allâmah Ṭabâṭabâ'î in *Shi'ite Islam*, translated and edited by S. H. Nasr, part II, section 3 (in press).

[24] See S. H. Nasr, *An Introduction to Islamic Cosmological Doctrines*, chapter I.

formed, and Sayyid Sharîf Murtaḍâ calls the Sufis 'real Shi'ites'.[25] The guilds and different orders of chivalry (*futuwwât*) also reveal a link between Shi'ism and Sufism because on the one hand they grew in a Shi'ite climate with particular devotion to 'Alî and on the other hand many of them became attached to Sufi orders and became extensions thereof in the form of 'craft initiations'.

After the Mongol invasion Shi'ism and Sufism once again formed a close association in many ways. Some of the Ismâ'îlîs, whose power had been broken by the Mongols, went underground and appeared later within Sufi orders or as new branches of already existing orders. In Twelve-Imâm Shi'ism also from the seventh/thirteenth to the tenth/sixteenth century Sufism began to grow within official Shi'ite circles. It was during this period that for the first time some of the Shi'ite *'ulamâ'* and jurisprudents were given such titles as *ṣûfî*, *'ârif* or *muta'allih*, and some of them devoted many pages of their writings to Sufi doctrines. Kamâl-al Dîn Maytham al-Baḥrânî in the seventh/thirteenth century wrote a commentary upon the *Nahj al-balâghah* revealing its gnostic and mystical meaning. Raḍî al-Dîn 'Alî ibn al-Ṭâ'ûs, a member of the well-known family of Shi'ite scholars and himself an outstanding Shi'ite *'âlim*, wrote prayers with Sufi connotations. 'Allâmah al-Ḥillî, the student of Naṣîr al-Dîn al-Ṭûsî and a person who played a great role in the spread of Shi'ism in Persia, has many works of gnostic character to his credit. Shortly after al-Ḥillî one of the most significant Shi'ite theologians of this period, Sayyid Ḥaydar Âmulî, was also a Sufi and follower of the school of Ibn 'Arabî. His *Jâmi' al-asrâr* is a summit of gnostic Shi'ism, where perhaps in more than any other work the metaphysical relationship between Shi'ism and Sufism is treated.[26] It is Âmulî who believed that every true Shi'ite is a Sufi and every true Sufi a Shi'ite.

The tendency toward the *rapprochement* between Sufism and official circles of Shi'ite learning and piety is to be seen in the ninth/fifteenth century in such figures as Hâfiẓ Rajab al-Bursî, author of the gnostic treatise *Mashâriq al-anwâr*, Ibn Abî Jumhûr, whose *Kitâb al-mujlî* is also a cornerstone of this new structure of Shi'ite gnostic literature and Kamâl al-Dîn Ḥusayn ibn 'Alî, entitled 'Wâ'iẓ-i Kâshifî'. The latter, although a Sunni, was a Naqshbandî Sufi and the author of Shi'ite devotional works which became extremely popular, especially the *Rawḍat al-shuhadâ'*, which has given its name

[25] See al-Shîbî, *al-Fikr al-shî'î . . .*, pp. 73 ff.

[26] This monumental work has been edited for the first time by H. Corbin and O. Yahya under the title of *La philosophie shi'ite* (see chapter VI, note 8) with an extensive introduction dealing with his life and ideas.

to the typically Shi'ite practice of *rawḍah* in which the martyrdom of Ḥusayn and other members of the household of the Prophet (*ahl al-bayt*) is celebrated. All these figures were instrumental in preparing the intellectual background for the Safavid renaissance which was based on both Shi'ism and Sufism.

Of special interest during this same period is the spread of the writings of Ibn 'Arabî in Persia and especially in Shi'ite circles.[27] It is well known that Ibn 'Arabî, from the point of view of his *madhhab*, was a Sunni of the Ẓâhirî school. But it is also known that he wrote a treatise on the twelve Shi'ite Imâms which has always been popular among Shi'ites.[28] There existed an inward complementarism and attraction between the writings of Ibn 'Arabî and Shi'ism which made the integration of his teachings into Shi'ite gnosis immediate and complete. Such Shi'ite Sufis as Sa'd al-Dîn Ḥamûyah, 'Abd al-Razzâq Kâshânî, Ibn Turkah, Sayyid Ḥaydar Âmulî and Ibn Abî Jumhûr, as well as many other Shi'ite gnostics of this period, are thoroughly impregnated with the teachings of Ibn 'Arabî, not to speak of the Shi'ite philosophers and theosophers, the culmination of whose thought is found in Mullâ Ṣadrâ and his school.

From the seventh/thirteenth to the tenth/sixteenth century there were also religious and Sufi movements which were linked with both Sufism and Shi'ism. The extremist sects of the *Ḥurûfîs* and the *Sha'sha'ah* grew directly out of a background that is both Shi'ite and Sufi.[29] More important in the long run than these sects were the Sufi orders that spread in Persia at this time and aided in preparing the ground for the Shi'ite movement of the Safavids. Two of these orders are of particular significance in this question of the relation between Shi'ism and Sufism: The Ni'matullâhî order and the Nûrbakhshî order. Shâh Ni'matullâh came originally from Aleppo and although a descendant of the Prophet was probably a Sunni in his *madhhab*.[30] But the order, which is closely akin to the Shâdhiliyyah order in its *silsilah* before Shâh Ni'matullâh, became a specifically Shi'ite Sufi order and remains to this day the most widespread Sufi order in the Shi'ite world. During the Safavid period it suffered an eclipse but underwent a major revival in the early Qajar era. The study of the

[27] See the previous chapter.

[28] This work, called the *Manâqib*, has also been commented upon in Persian. See Mûsâ Khalkhâlî, *Sharḥ manâqib Muḥyî al-Dîn ibn 'Arabî*, Tehran, 1322.

[29] See al-Shîbî, *al-Fikr al-shî'î . . .*, pp. 179–244, 302-27.

[30] Concerning his life and works see I. Aubin, *Materiaux pour la biographie de Shâh Ni'matollâh Walî Kermânî*, Tehran-Paris, 1956 and the several studies devoted to him by J. Nourbakhsh, the present *Quṭb* of the order, published by the Ni-'matullâhî *Khâniqâh* in Tehran during the last decade.

doctrines and methods of this order, which possesses a regularity of chain or *silsilah* and method very much similar to the Sufi orders in the Sunni world, is most revealing as an example of a still living order of Sufism that is thoroughly Shi'ite and functions in a Shi'ite climate.

The Nûrbakhshî order, founded by Muḥammad ibn 'Abdallâh, entitled Nûrbakhsh, a Persian from Quhistan, is particularly interesting in that the founder sought to create a kind of bridge between Sunnism and Shi'ism in his own person and gave a Mahdiist colour to his movement.[31] The spread of his order and the power of his personality were instrumental in drawing many people to hold particular reverence for 'Alî and the 'Alids. His own open declaration was that his movement combined Sufism and Shi'ism.[32] And the spread of his ideas was one of the factors that brought forth this combination of Shi'ism and Sufi movements which resulted in the Safavid domination of Iran.[33]

In the Ottoman Empire also one can observe the close association between Shi'ism and Sufism in the Baktâshî order, founded by a Khurâsânî, Ḥâjj Baktâsh, who after fleeing from the Tartars found numerous disciples among the Persians and Anatolian Turks and established the order which exercised so much influence during the Ottoman period.[34] Although with the establishment of a Shi'ite Persia by the Safavids the Shi'ites were severely persecuted in the Ottoman Empire, the Baktâshî order continued to display strong Shi'ite tendencies and possessed, and in fact continues to possess, a spiritual atmosphere very similar to what one finds in certain Sufi orders in the Shi'ite world.

The rise of the Safavids from the nucleus of the Sufi order of Shaykh Ṣafî al-Dîn Ardibîlî is too well known to need repetition here.[35] Suffice it to say that this political movement which founded the new Persian state was Sufi in origin and Shi'ite in belief. As a result it made

[31] Concerning Shaykh Nûrbakhsh and also the Kubrawiyyah and their importance in connection with Persia's becoming Shi'ite see the articles of M. Molé in the *Revue des études islamiques* from 1959 to 1963.

[32] The text of his declaration is quoted by al-Shîbî, *al-Fikr al-shî'î*. . . , p. 335.

[33] Concerning the different Sufi orders in the Shi'ite climate of Persia see M. Molé, *Les mystiques musulmans*, chapter IV.

[34] Concerning the Baktâshîs and their affiliation with Shi'ism see J. Birge, *The Bektâshî Order of Dervishes*, London, 1937, chapter VI.

[35] Based on the original historic sources such as *'Âlam ârâ-yi 'abbâsî* and *Rawḍat al-ṣafâ'*, many historical works have been devoted to the origin of the Safavids by such scholars as Minorsky, Togan, Hinz, Aubin, Savory and others. See for example Z. V. Togan, 'Sur l'origines des safavides', *Mélanges Louis Massignon*, Paris, 1957, vol. 3, pp. 345–57. The work of W. Hinz, *Irans Aufstieg zum Nationalstaat im fünfzehnten Jahrhundert*, Berlin, 1936, is of particular value for its historical analysis.

Shi'ism the official religion of Persia while aiding the growth and propagation of Sufi ideas at least in the earlier period of its rule. It is not, therefore, surprising to see during this period a renaissance of Shi'ite learning in which Shi'ite gnosis plays such an important role. The names of Mîr Dâmâd, Mîr Findiriskî, Ṣadr al-Din Shîrâzî, Mullâ Muḥsin Fayḍ, 'Abd al-Razzâq Lâhîjî, Qâḍî Sa'îd Qumî, Mullâ Na'îmâ Ṭâliqânî and so many other gnostics of this period perhaps belong more to the chapter on Safavid theosophy and philosophy than to Sufism,[36] but since all these men were Shi'ite and at the same time completely impregnated with Sufi gnostic ideas, they represent yet another facet of the connection between Shi'ism and Sufism. There were also outstanding Shi'ite *'ulamâ'* of this period who were practising Sufis like Bahâ' al-Dîn 'Âmilî and Muḥammad Taqî Majlisî as well as masters of regular Sufi orders like the Dhahabîs, Ni'matullâhîs and Safavis.[37]

Strangely enough, however, during the reign of the same dynasty whose origin was Sufi a severe reaction set in against the Sufi orders partly because, due to royal patronage of Sufism, many extraneous elements had joined it for worldly ends and also because some of the orders became lax in their practice of the *Sharî'ah.* Some of the religious scholars wrote treatises against the Sufis such as *al-Fawâ'id al-dîniyyah fi'l-radd 'ala'l-ḥukamâ' wa'l-ṣûfiyyah* by Mullâ Muḥammad Ṭâhir Qumî. Even the outstanding theologian and scholar, Mullâ Muḥammad Bâqir Majlisî, who was not completely against Sufism as attested by his *Zâd al-ma'âd*, was forced in these circumstances to deny his own father's Sufism and openly oppose the Sufis. In such a climate Sufism encountered a great deal of difficulty during the latter part of the Safavid era and in this period even the theosophers (*ḥukamâ'*) of the school of Mullâ Ṣadrâ faced severe opposition from some of the *'ulamâ'*. It was as a result of this situation that in religious circles Sufism henceforth changed its name to *'irfân* and to this day in the official Shi'ite religious circles and *madrasahs*, one can openly study, teach and discuss *'irfân* but never *taṣawwuf*, which is too often associated with the indisciplined and lax dervishes oblivious to the injunctions of the *Sharî'ah* who are usually called *qalandar ma'âb* in Persian.

[36] Concerning these figures see S. H. Nasr, 'The School of Ispahan' and 'Ṣadr al-Dîn Shîrâzî' in M. M. Sharif (ed.), *A History of Muslim Philosophy*, vol. II, Wiesbaden, 1966, and H. Corbin, 'Confessions extatiques de Mîr Dâmâd', *Mélanges Louis Massignon*, pp. 331–78.

[37] See Sayyid 'Abd al-Ḥujjat Balâghî, *Maqalat al-ḥunafâ' fî maqâmât Shams al-'Urafâ'*.

During the ensuing Afghan invasion and the reestablishment of a strong government by Nâdir Shâh there was not much talk of Sufism in Shi'ite circles in Persia while Sufism prospered in Shi'ite milieus in India. And it is from the Deccan that in the twelfth/eighteenth century Ma'ṣûm 'Alî Shâh and Shâh Ṭâhir of the Ni'matullâhî order were sent to Persia to revive Sufism. Although some of their disciples like Nûr 'Alî Shâh and Muẓaffar 'Alî Shâh were martyred,[38] Sufism began to flourish once again, especially during the rule of the Qajar king Fatḥ 'Alî Shâh, while Muḥammad Shâh and his prime minister, Ḥâjj Mîrzâ Âqâsî, were themselves attracted to Sufism. Henceforth the different Sufi orders, especially the various branches of the Ni'matullâhî, as well as the Dhahabî and Khâksâr, flourished in Shi'ite Persia and continue to do so now. Also during the Qajar period, the gnostic doctrines of Ibn 'Arabî and Ṣadr al-Dîn Shîrâzî were revived by such men as Ḥâjjî Mullâ Hâdî Sabziwârî and Âqâ Muḥammad Riḍâ Qumsha'î;[39] their school still continues to thrive at the present time.

Today in the Shi'ite world and particularly Shi'ite Persia one can distinguish between three groups of gnostics and mystics: those who belong to regular Sufi orders such as the Ni'matullâhî or the Dhahabî and who follow a way very similar to those of Sufis in the Sunni world; those who also have had a definite spiritual master and have received regular initiation but whose master and those before him do not constitute an organized and 'institutionalized' Sufi order with an openly declared *silsilah* and established centre or *khâniqâh*; and finally those who have definitely received a gnostic and mystical inspiration and have authentic visions (*mushâhadah*) and experience spiritual states (*aḥwâl*), but who do not possess a human master. Of this latter group some are Uwaysîs, others belong to the line of *Khaḍir* or *Khiḍr* in Persian,[40] and most reach spiritual contact with the Imâm who is also the inner spiritual guide. The overflow of esotericism in

[38] Concerning these figures see R. Gramlich, *Die schiitischen Derwischorden Persiens, Erster Teil: Die Affiliationen*, Wiesbaden, 1965, pp, 33 ff.

[39] See S. H. Nasr, 'Sabziwârî', in *A History of Muslim Philosophy*, vol. II, and the Introduction of T. Izutsu, 'The Fundamental Structure of Sabziwarian Metaphysics', to Sabziwârî, *Sharḥ-i manẓûmah*, ed. by M. Mohaghegh and T. Izutsu, Tehran, 1969.

[40] On the spiritual significance of Khaḍir or Khiḍr see L. Massignon, 'Elie et son rôle transhistorique, Khaḍirîya en Islam', *Etudes carmélitaines: Elie le prophète*, vol. II, Paris, 1956, pp. 269–90. Massignon has also devoted numerous other articles to this subject most of which have appeared in the *Revue des études islamiques*. There are also many valuable references to initiation in Sufism through Khiḍr and to the *afrâd* who have received such initiation in the writings of R. Guénon on initiation.

Shi'ism into even the more outward aspects of the religion has made this third type of possibility more common here than one would find in Sunni Islam. Some of the great theosophers and gnostics in fact, who have definitely reached the state of spiritual vision as attested by their works, belong to this latter category and also perhaps to the second category because in that case likewise it is difficult to discern the spiritual lineage outwardly.

Shi'ism and Sufism, then, possess a common parentage in that they are both linked with the esoteric dimension of the Islamic revelation and in their earliest history drew inspiration from the same sources. In later periods they have had many mutual interactions and influenced each other in innumerable ways. But these historical manifestations have been no more than applications to different moments of time of an essential and principial relationship which belongs to the eternal and integral reality of Islam itself and which in the form of the gnosis that characterizes Islamic esotericism has manifested itself in both segments of the Islamic community, the Sunni and Shi'ite alike.

PART III

IX

Islam and the Encounter of Religions

إنا أنزلنا التورية فيها هدى ونور يحكم بها النبيون لذين أسلموا
للذين هادوا والربانيون والأحبار بما استحفظوا من كتاب الله وكانوا
عليه شهداء فلاتخشو الناس واخشون ولاتشتروا بآياتى ثمناً قليلاً ومن لم
يحكم بما أنزل الله فأولئك هم الكافرون

Lo! We did reveal the Torah, wherein is guidance and a light, by which the Prophets who surrendered (unto Allah) judged the Jews, and the rabbis and the priests (judged) by such of Allah's Scriptures as they were bidden to observe, and thereunto were they witnesses. So fear not mankind, but fear Me. And barter not My revelations for a little gain. Whoso judgeth not by that which Allah hath revealed: such are disbelievers.

(Quran, V, 44)

اختلاف خلق از نام اوفتاد چون به معنى رفت آرام اوفتاد
ازنظر گاه است اى مغز وجود اختلاف مؤمن وگبر ويهود

The difference among creatures comes from the outward form (*nâm*);
When one penetrates into the inner meaning (*ma'nâ*) there is peace.
Oh marrow of existence! It is because of the point of view in question
That there has come into being differences among the Muslim, Zoroastrian and Jew.

(Rûmî)

I

Because it is concerned with the inner meaning (*ma'nâ*) through the penetration of the outward form (*nâm*), Sufism is by nature qualified to delve into the mysterious unity that underlies the diversity of religious forms. It is, moreover, the only aspect of Islam that can do full justice to the more profound questions of comparative religion, questions which cannot be ignored without violating the nature of religion itself. Moreover, the spread of modern influences into the Islamic world has made a serious study of comparative religion into an imperative need; the way to meet this need is to make use of all the keys stored in the treasury of Sufi wisdom wherewith to open doors which would otherwise remain locked and thus help to solve many intellectual problems by drawing on the metaphysical insight provided by the esoteric teachings of Islam as contained in Sufism.

In considering the problem of comparative religion from the Islamic point of view, it must be remembered at the outset that the metaphysical and theological significance of the presence of other religions differs depending on whether one is considering homogeneous traditional civilizations or the modern world, in which a homogeneous world view is no longer to be found. For traditional man, Muslim or otherwise, that is, a man whose life and thought are moulded by a set of principles of transcendent origin and who lives in a society in which these principles are manifested in every sphere, other religious traditions appear as alien worlds which do not concern him as an immediate spiritual reality save in exceptional cases which only go to prove the rule. Before modern times the founder of each religion appeared as the sun in the solar system in which his followers were born, lived and died. The founders of other religions were either not known—just as when the sun shines one can no longer observe the stars, which are nevertheless suns in their own right—or in certain cases such as that of Islam itself they were relegated to the rank of stars in the firmament, which do not have the same significance as the sun although they too are suns at the centre of their own solar systems.

Just as man is mentally and psychologically constituted in such a way as to live in a physical world with only one sun, even if modern astronomy assures him of the presence of others, so he is constituted religiously and spiritually to live under the light of the particular sun who is the founder of the religion to which he belongs. In normal times a man's religion is *the* religion, and in fact each religion addresses itself to a humanity which, for it, is humanity as such. The exclusiveness of a religion is a symbol of its divine origin, of the fact that it comes from the Absolute, of its being in itself a total way of life. Under normal circumstances there would be no need to take cognizance of the metaphysical significance of other traditions, just as normally man needs only to know of the sun of his own solar system in order to live a normal life on earth. Even if modern astronomy teaches him that there are myriads of other suns in the Universe, he relegates this knowledge to the background of his mind and continues to live as if his sun were the only one. The immediate experience of the physical world in which he lives presents to him a picture that has something absolute in its nature because of its symbolic content. Man was created to live in precisely such a world where there is only one sun in the sky so that the normal appearance of a single sun in the firmament corresponds to the natural structure of man's mind and psyche, and alone constitutes a natural and meaningful environment for him.

Likewise, in the religious sphere, man has been created to live in a homogeneous religious tradition, one in which the values of his religion are for him *the* values, absolute and binding. As long as the traditional divisions of humanity continued to subsist it was unnecessary, or, one might even say redundant, to seek to penetrate into the meaning of other traditions except in the particular circumstances when two religious traditions came in direct contact with one other. But even here the significance of this encounter was not the same as it is today when the homogeneity of the traditional climate itself is broken in the West and to a greater or lesser extent in other parts of the world where the modernist outlook has taken root. For centuries Christian and Jewish minorities have lived within the Islamic world and there has been even occasional religious contact between the respective communities; but each community has lived in its own traditional world. The necessity for the study of one tradition by another in such a case has not been at all the same as that faced by a modern educated person who, having been touched by the effect of modern thought, is forced to consider the problems of other religions on a different basis, a basis which concerns the nature of religion itself.

It might then be said that the necessity for studying other religious traditions is brought about by the particular conditions of the modern world, where the bounds of both the astronomical and religious universe have been broken. The dilemma of wishing to be able to remain faithful to one's own religion and yet come to accept the validity of other traditions is one of the results of the abnormal conditions that modern man faces and is a consequence of the anomalous conditions in which he lives. Yet it is a problem that he must face on pain of losing faith in religion itself. For a traditional Muslim living in Fez or Mashhad it is not necessary to be concerned with the verities of Buddhism or Christianity. Nor is it urgent for a peasant in the hills of Italy or Spain to learn about Hinduism. But for a person for whom the homogeneity of a religious culture has been ruptured by modern secularist philosophies or, alternatively, affected by contact with the authentic spirituality of foreign traditions, it is no longer possible to ignore the metaphysical and theological implications of the presence of other religions. If he does so, he falls into the danger of either losing his own religion or having a conception of the Divinity which, to say the least, places a limit upon the Divine Mercy.

The very plurality of religious forms has been used by some as an argument against the validity of all religions. The insistance upon this view, stated in so many different forms today, itself proves the urgency of the study of other religions today for the sake of preserving religion itself. Moreover, this task is placed upon the shoulders of either those who have come into contact with the modern mentality and yet remain spiritually inclined, or else of those who thanks to exceptional circumstances are enabled to carry out this task. Traditional authorities are completely within their rights to address a traditional audience without the need of referring to other religious forms. But there are also those whose vocation it is to provide the keys with which the treasury of wisdom of other traditions can be unlocked, revealing to those who are destined to receive this wisdom the essential unity and universality and at the same time the formal diversity of tradition and revelation.[1] The most powerful defence for religion in the face of modern scepticism is precisely the universality of religion, the realization of the basic truth that God has addressed man many times, in each case saying 'I' and speaking in a language that is suitable for the particular humanity to which the revelation is addressed.[2]

The difficulty of studying the relation between religions seriously arises, of course, only when one is concerned with the truth of religion itself. For the sceptic or the 'scientific' observer or the syncretist the problem never transcends that of historical events and phenomena or

[1] Several authors in the West have, in fact, during the past half-century presented to the world this cardinal teaching, men like Réné Guénon, Ananda Coomaraswamy, Titus Burckhardt, Marco Pallis, Martin Lings, and especially Frithjof Schuon, whose many works, particularly *The Transcendent Unity of Religions*, have revealed with unparalleled lucidity the essential unity and, at the same time, the formal diversity of the great traditions of the world. It is a tragedy for the academic discipline of comparative religion that except for a very few cases no serious attention has been paid to these writings.

On another level one may mention the works of such scholars as Mircea Eliade, Heinrich Zimmer, Jean Herbert, Eugen Herrigel, Rudolf Otto, Henry Corbin and Louis Massignon, whose findings contribute much to a genuine understanding of other religions. Also among Catholic authors or those sympathetic to the point of view of Catholicism such figures as Simone Weil, Bernard Kelly, Elémire Zolla and Dom A. Graham speak in a language which has contributed profitably to an effective discourse between religions. See W. Stoddart, 'Catholicism and Zen', *Tomorrow*, vol. XII, no. 4, Autumn, 1964, pp. 289–96.

[2] The Holy Quran says 'And We never sent a messenger save with the language of his folk, that he might make (the message) clear for them' (XIV. 4).

of sentimental attitudes; it is not with such an approach that we are concerned here. The essential problem that the study of religion poses is how to preserve religious truth, traditional orthodoxy, the dogmatic theological structures of one's own religion and yet gain knowledge of other traditions and accept them as spiritually valid ways and roads to God. For one who is colour-blind it matters little what colours make up the rainbow. And it is precisely here that the very forces that have made the study of other religions religiously and metaphysically necessary have also made such a study difficult.

Modernism has either destroyed religious faith or else has narrowed it. Men of old were not only less sceptical than modern man but also less narrow in their faith. Today everyone congratulates himself on having an open mind; one can agree that it is good to have the windows of the mind open provided the mind also has walls. If a room has no walls it does not matter very much whether the windows are open or closed. Once man rejects revelation and tradition there is little virtue in religious open-mindedness because there is no longer a criterion for distinguishing the true from the false. Faith has narrowed in the case of many Christians as well as Muslims, Hindus, and others; here one is speaking, not about those who have fallen outside of the tradition, and therefore have no faith either narrow or broad, but about those who remain within it, but whose religious faith has become narrowly constricted as a result of the onslaught of modernism. Just to cite the case of Islam, modernism has not only caused some men to have their faith weakened but it has also produced certain movements against the most universal aspect of Islam, namely Sufism. Often a simple peasant has a more universal conception of Islam than a university-educated rationalist.

Another difficulty that modernism places in the way of a serious study of other religions is its own negation of the very metaphysical principles that underlie all religions. The 'science' of comparative religion or *Religionswissenschaft* began during the age of rationalism and came into its own as a separate discipline during the nineteenth century. The history of this discipline carries with it the limitations and prejudices of the period of its formation.[3] The 'age of enlightenment' saw itself as the final perfection of civilization and studied other religions as a prelude to Christianity with which it somehow identified itself despite its own rebellion against the Christian tradition. This

[3] For an account of the phases that the discipline of comparative religion has undergone and the influences that have shaped it see M. Eliade, 'The Quest for the "Origins" of Religion', *History of Religions*, vol. IV, no. 1, Summer, 1964, pp. 156 ff.

attitude has continued to subsist to a certain degree. That is why to this day Islam receives the least satisfactory treatment at the hands of those interested in comparative religion. Coming after Christianity, it simply does not fit into the pre-conceived pattern that other religions were simple and childish imitations of something that reached its perfection with Christianity through the process of evolution, which everything is supposed somehow to undergo.[4]

Likewise, the nineteenth century left its own mark upon this discipline by impregnating it with theories of linear historical progress and the like, as well as the theory mentioned above, these being the best guarantee of not understanding a religious tradition and its spiritual significance. Phenomenology, which has criticized the shortcomings of the historical method and emphasized the morphological study of all religious manifestations, has been in a sense an improvement, but even that has not been sufficient. What has been lacking is true metaphysics, which alone can reveal the transparency of forms and bring to light their inner meaning. The study of religions began in the West when, on the one hand, the true metaphysical aspect of the Christian tradition had become eclipsed and nearly forgotten and, on the other hand, secular philosophies had become dominant which were from the beginning opposed to the very idea of the Transcendent and the *scientia sacra* which lies hidden within every religion. The study of religions, therefore, has been coloured by the mentality of modern Western man and seen under categories which have been either borrowed from later developments of Christianity or from reactions against Christianity.[5] But in any case that metaphysical

[4] 'So little is the Western historian of religions nowadays equipped in Islamics that that discipline, to which he has hardly contributed anything, does not seem to need him. Even today, no historian of religions proper has had anything to say that would catch the attention of the men of knowledge in the Islamics field.' Isma'il R. A. al-Faruqi, 'History of Religions: Its nature and significance for Christian education and the Muslim-Christian Dialogue', *Numen*, vol. XII, fasc. 1, Jan., 1965, p. 40.

Some may object to this statement by pointing to men like W. C. Smith or R. C. Zaehner who have made well-known contributions to Islamic and Iranian studies. But such men were in fact first Islamicists and Iranologists and only later went into the field of the history of religions.

[5] There has been some study of other religions by Hindus as well, but for the most part by modernized Hindus who have usually expounded a shallow 'universalism' which can only end in a mere humanitarianism or in the pseudo-spiritual cults which have sprung up everywhere in the West today. Even some genuine Hindu *bhaktas* have contributed to this situation because once out of their traditional environment, which 'thinks' for them, they do not have the power of discernment to be able to distinguish between the multitude of forms in civilizations which are alien to them.

background which is indispensable for a study in depth of religion has generally been lacking.

It is not, therefore, without interest for the discipline of comparative religion itself to see how the problem of the encounter of religions is seen from the point of view of other traditions. Such a knowledge provides one more vision of a reality which surrounds us, but it is a vision from another perspective than the familiar one, and therefore reveals another aspect of this encompassing reality. Whatever any orthodox religion has to say about the relation between religions is itself a precious insight into the real nature of religion as such and helps to explain the juxtaposition of religions in the spiritual space in which they are situated. It is with this end in view that the study of the problem of the encounter of religions from the Islamic point of view can be fruitful, since in this way it will also be possible to bring into focus the metaphysical and theological implications of the presence of other religious traditions for Islam itself.

The metaphysical background which was absent when the study of comparative religion began in the West has always been alive within the Islamic tradition as within other living Oriental traditions. According to it reality is comprised not of just the single psycho-physical level in which ordinary men live but of multiple states of being standing hierarchically one above the other. Each state of being possesses its own objective reality, the degree of its reality depending on how intense is the light of Being which illuminates it. At the origin stands the source of all existence, the Absolute which is at once Being and above-Being (the *dhât* of Sufism). The basis of all metaphysical doctrine is the distinction between the Absolute and the relative. The task of all traditional cosmology is to elucidate the science of forms belonging to each state of being. In Islam all metaphysics is contained in the first *Shahâdah*, *Lâ ilâha ill'Allâh* (there is no divinity but the Divine), which means ultimately that only the Absolute is absolute, all else is relative; and all cosmology is contained in principle in the second *Shahâdah*, *Muḥammadun rasûl Allâh* (Muḥammad is the messenger of God), which means that all that is positive in the Universe, of which Muḥammad is the supreme symbol, comes from God.

If then the source of all things, all beings, all forms, is the Transcendent Reality, every being must have an external and an internal aspect, one which manifests it outwardly and another which connects it inwardly to the spiritual world. It is said in the Quran that God is both the Outward (*al-ẓâhir*) and the Inward (*al-bâṭin*). One might also say, using the language of Sufism, that each thing in the Universe has an outward form (*ṣûrah*) and an inner essence (*ma'nâ*). The form belongs to the world of multiplicity and the essence leads to Unity which is the Origin of all things. This is especially true of religion, that direct manifestation of the Divine in the human order. It too must have a form and an essence. And so religions can be studied either in their forms, which should then be described and compared, or in their essence, which leads to their inner unity because the source of all reality and therefore all religion is God who is One. But inasmuch as the essence comes before the form and links it with the higher orders of being it is precisely through the essence that the significance of the form can be understood. Only by gaining a vision of Unity can man come to realize the unity of all that exists. Only in understanding the essence of a religion can its forms become understood as intelligible symbols rather than opaque facts.

Islam's relation to other religions has been dictated by this metaphysical doctrine which underlies its whole intellectual edifice. It has studied both the forms of other religions and, in certain instances, their essence. And today it stands equipped with the necessary intellectual and spiritual means of carrying out this study in the new circumstances which the modern world has placed before it.

A characteristic of Islam which is particularly pertinent in regard to this question is the synthesizing and integrating power of the Islamic revelation, which allows the grace of the prophets and saints of previous religions—especially of the Abrahamic line—to reach the Muslim within the context provided by the grace of the Prophet of Islam. For a Christian all the grace of God is centred in the personality of Christ, without whom there would be no other channel of grace open to man. For the Muslim, within the firmament of Islam, in which the Prophet is like the full moon, other great prophets and saints are like stars which shine in the same firmament, but they do so by virtue of the grace of Muḥammad—upon whom be peace. A Muslim can pray to Abraham or Christ, not as Jewish or Christian prophets, but as Muslim ones, and in fact often does so, as seen in the popular 'prayer of Abraham' in the Sunni world and the *Du'â-yi wârith* in Shi'ite Islam. The synthesizing power of Islam has made possible the integration of previous spiritual poles within the world of Islam and the effective operation of their particular grace within that world. This feature of Islam, so important in the ritual life of Muslims, has also the greatest significance in the intellectual and spiritual aspects of the problem of comparative religion from the Islamic point of view.

II

At first sight it may seem strange that, despite the features described above, Islam is, of all the major religions of the world today, the one that has displayed the least amount of interest in the study of the history and doctrines of other religions although its own point of view about religion is the most universal possible. Very few works have been written in this field in Persian and even fewer in Arabic except for translations from European sources.[6] And in recently established programmes in the field of religion in America and England there are fewer Muslim students than those of any other major tradition.

The reason for this relative neglect of the discipline of comparative religion by Muslims is that Islam is not at all disturbed theologically by the presence of other religions. The existence of other traditions is taken for granted, and in fact Islam is based on the conception of the universality of revelation. The Quran among all sacred scriptures is the one that speaks the most universal language,[7] and Muslims believe in the existence of a large number of prophets (traditionally given as 124,000) sent to every people.[8] The spiritual anthropology depicted in the Quran makes of prophecy a necessary element of the human condition. Man is truly man only by virtue of his participation in a tradition. Adam, the first man, was also the first prophet. Man did not evolve from polytheism to monotheism. He began as a monotheist and has to be gradually reminded of the original message of unity

[6] Although the author's own knowledge of the situation of other Muslim languages is limited, the same seems to be true of Turkish, Urdu, etc., except that naturally in Urdu, Bengali and other languages of the Muslims of the Indo-Pakistani sub-continent many works can be found concerning Hindu religion and culture. But even here, since the partition of the sub-continent, very few works of substance free from transient factors and sentimental considerations have seen the light of day. The Urdu language is rich in works dealing with Hinduism, including not only translations of Hindu sacred texts (mostly from translations that had been made previously into Persian), but also new works on different aspects of Hinduism written often by Hindus themselves but in Urdu. Some Muslims also have written outstanding expositions of Hindu doctrines, such as the work of Ḥabîb al-Raḥmân Shastri composed in 1930 on the theory of *rasa*, which received very favourable comments from Hindu circles. But nearly all of these works belong also to the last decades of the last century and the early period of this century. See M. H. Askari, 'Tradition et modernisme dans le monde indo-pakistanais', *Etudes Traditionnelles*, May-June and July-August 1970, pp. 98–125.

[7] The Holy Quran states: 'And for every nation there is a messenger' (X, 48).

[8] This large number of prophets indicates implicitly that all nations must have been given a religion sent to them by God. Although generally only the Abrahamic tradition has been considered, the principle of the universality of revelation applies to all nations, and Muslims applied it outside the Abrahamic family when faced with Zoroastrianism in Persia and Hinduism in India.

(*al-tawḥîd*) which he is ever in danger of forgetting. Human history consists of cycles of prophecy, with each new prophecy beginning a new cycle of humanity.

Islam also considers itself to be the reassertion of the original religion, of the doctrine of Unity, which always was and always will be. That is why it is called the primordial religion (*al-dîn al-ḥanîf*); it comes at the end of this human cycle to reassert the essential truth of the primordial tradition.[9] It is thus like the *sanâtana dharma* of Hinduism, and on the metaphysical plane has a profound affinity with this tradition, which some Sufis have in fact called the '*Sharî'ah* or religion of Adam'. Not only have some of the most authoritative Muslim scholars of the sub-continent during the Moghul period called the Hindus '*ahl al-kitâb*', belonging to the chain of prophets preceding Islam and beginning with Adam, but also some of the Muslim Indian commentators have considered the prophet Dhu'l-Kifl mentioned in the Quran to be the Buddha of Kifl (Kapilavasta) and the 'Fig Tree' of surah 95 to be the Bodi Tree under which the Buddha received his illumination. Muslims have always had an innate feeling of possessing in their purest form the doctrines that all religions have come to proclaim before. In Islamic gnosis, or Sufism, this truth is *al-tawḥîd* in its metaphysical sense, the eternal wisdom, the *religio perennis*, which Islam has come to reveal in its fullness. For the Shari'ite Muslim it is the doctrine of monotheism which he believes to have been revealed by every prophet. That is why at the end of the cycle the appearance of the Mahdî brings to light the common inner meaning of all religions.

These and other more contingent factors have made Muslims less interested in the study of other religions than is the case with Christians, Hindus and others. But nevertheless it is necessary today to remind the modern educated Muslims of the universality of their own tradition and of the historical contacts Islam has made with other religions, a fact that has been gradually forgotten in recent times in many circles. Moreover it is necessary to apply the universal principles contained within Islam to study other traditions in the light of the anomalous conditions that the modern world has brought about.[10]

[9] See F. Schuon, *Understanding Islam*, chapter I.

[10] One cannot overlook the fact that there are some—although still few in number—among Westernized Muslims who, in their extreme degree of Westernization, have also begun to take an interest in Hinduism, Zen, and other oriental disciplines, but usually of the spurious kind. For them also a direct and authentic contact between Islam and these traditions can be of the greatest aid in becoming oriented spiritually. There are a few who have had direct contact with authorities belonging to these traditions, but their number is extremely limited.

To understand the encounter of Islam with other religions it must be remembered that Islam itself comprises an exoteric and an esoteric dimension, namely a Divine Law or *Sharî'ah* and a spiritual way or *Ṭarîqah*. Moreover Islam has cultivated different arts and sciences and intellectual perspectives. It has its own schools of theology, philosophy and theosophy (*ḥikmah*)—understood in its original sense before modern usage had debased the word. It has had its own historians and scholars, geographers and travellers. Through all of these channels Islam has encountered other religions, and the profundity of the encounter has depended each time on the perspective in question.

If we exclude the modern period with its rapid means of communication, it can be said with safety that Islam has had more contact with other traditions than any other of the world religions. It encountered Christianity and Judaism in its cradle and during its first expansion northward. It met the Iranian religions, both Zoroastrianism and Manichaeism, in the Sassanid Empire. It gradually absorbed small communities in which remnants of late Hellenistic cults continued, especially the Sabaean community of Harran, which considered itself the heir to the most esoteric aspect of the Greek tradition. It met Buddhism in north-west Persia, Afghanistan, and Central Asia, and Hinduism in Sind and later in many parts of the Indian sub-continent. There was even contact with Mongolian and Siberian Shamanism on the popular level, mostly through the Turkish tribes who had followed Shamanism before their conversion to Islam. Moreover the Muslims of Sinkiang were in direct contact with the Chinese tradition.

In fact, of all the important religious traditions of Asia—putting aside Shintoism which was limited to Japan—there is none with which Muslims have had no early intellectual contact, save for the Chinese tradition with which contact on a religious and intellectual level by the main part of the Muslim world happened only after the Mongol invasion. As for the Chinese Muslim Community, it remained more or less separated from its coreligionists further West so that its knowledge of the Chinese tradition was not generally shared. Only an occasional traveller like Ibn Baṭṭûṭah provided the Muslim intelligentsia with a knowledge of things Chinese. Yet, even with regard to the Chinese tradition the Muslims preserved a sense of respect. The prophetic *ḥadîth* 'Seek knowledge, even in China' was known by all, and some Persian Sufis have made specific reference to the Divine origin of the Chinese tradition. Farîd al-Dîn 'Aṭṭâr in his *Manṭiq al-ṭayr* (*Conference of the Birds*), speaking of the Sîmurgh who symbolizes the Divine Essence and his feather which symbolizes divine revelation, writes:

'An astonishing thing! The first manifestation of the Sîmurgh took place in China in the middle of the night. One of his feathers fell on China and his reputation filled the world. Everyone made a picture of this feather, and from it formed his own system of ideas, and so fell into a turmoil. This feather is still in the picture-gallery of that country; hence the saying, "Seek knowledge, even in China!"

'But for his manifestation there would not have been so much noise in the world concerning this mysterious Being. This sign of his existence is a token of his glory. All souls carry an impression of the image of his feather. Since the description of it has neither head nor tail, beginning nor end, it is not necessary to say more about it.'[11]

As for the encounter of Islam with the Judaeo-Christian tradition, this has persisted throughout nearly fourteen centuries of the history of Islam. Judaism and Christianity themselves are in a sense 'contained' in Islam inasmuch as the latter is the final affirmation of the Abrahamic tradition of which Judaism and Christianity are the two earlier manifestations. However there is no question of historical borrowing here as some orientalists have sought to show; the *Sharî'ah* is a Divine Law similar in many ways to Talmudic law, but not borrowed from it or based upon it; Christ plays a very important role in Islam, but this is not a distortion of the Christian conception of Christ. The latter is, independently of Christianity, a part of the Islamic religious view. Christ and Moses, as well as the other ancient Hebrew prophets, play a part in Islam independently of any possible historical borrowing from Judaism and Christianity. The similarities that exist come only from the common transcendent archetype of Judaism, Christianity and Islam.

Encounters with Judaism and Christianity during the early Islamic centuries were mostly polemical and concerned with theological questions; it can, in fact, be said that the problems faced by Philo and the early Church Fathers, versus the rational demonstration of articles of faith such as the immortality of the soul, resurrection of the body and creation *ex-nihilo*, influenced early Muslim theologians in adopting similar arguments for the defence of Islam against rationalistic

[11] Farîd ud-Dîn Aṭṭâr, *The Conference of the Birds*, trans. S. C. Nott, London, 1954, p. 13. See also H. Ritter, *Das Meer der Seele*, Leiden, 1955, pp. 607–8.

criticism.[12] Usually most of the early Muslim works on the history of religion (*al-Milal wa'l-niḥal*) contain chapters devoted to Judaism and Christianity, some of which like *al-Mughnī* of Qâḍî 'Abd al-Jabbâr are precious documents for present-day knowledge of certain aspects of the Eastern Church and of the eastern Christian communities. The figures of Moses and Christ appear in nearly every Muslim religious work, especially those of the Sufis, such as the *Futûḥât al-makkiyyah* of Ibn 'Arabî, the *Mathnawî* of Rûmî, or the *Gulshan-i râz* of Shabistarî. Nearly every experience undergone by these prophets, such as the vision of the burning bush by Moses, or Christ's miracle of raising the dead to life, plays an important part in the exposition of Sufi doctrine.[13] Needless to say, all these sources rejected the ideas of divine filiation and incarnation in Christianity, neither of which ideas is in conformity with the Islamic perspective, and occasionally works were written with the express purpose of refuting these doctrines.[14]

It must not be thought that contact between the Muslim and the Christian and Jewish communities has been constant over the ages. During the first centuries of Islam, especially the early Abbasid period, debates between the different communities were common. After the

[12] The many writings of H. A. Wolfson, especially his *Philo* and his *Philosophy o the Kalâm*, have amply demonstrated the result of this interaction between Jewish, Christian, and Muslim theologians and the influence of Judaeo—Christian theological arguments upon the *Kalâm* itself.

[13] Christ is given the supreme position of the universal 'Seal of Sanctity' (*Khâtam al-wilâyah*) and is believed to be the one who will bring the cycle to a close after the advent of the Mahdî. Ibn 'Arabî writes of Christ in his *Futûḥât* (VI, 215):

> Oui, le Sceau des Saints est un Apôtre
> Qui n'aura point d'égal dans le monde!
> Il est l'Esprit et il est le fils de l'Esprit et de la mère Marie
> C'est là un rang qu'aucun autre ne pourra atteindre.
> Il descendra parmi nous en arbitre juste
> Mais non point selon les principes de sa propre loi qui aura cessé
> Il tuera le porc et confondra l'iniquité;
> Allah sera seul son guide. . . .

M. Hayek, *Le Christ de l'Islam*, Paris, 1959, p. 260.

[14] An outstanding example of a work of this kind is al-Ghazzâlî's refutation of the divinity of Christ, in which, using the text of the Gospels, he argued that Christ was given special permission by God—a permission that is unique among prophets —to use the type of language that he employed concerning his union and filial relationship with God, but that in reality he never attributed divinity to himself as is commonly understood by Christians. See al-Ghazzâlî, *Réfutation excéllente de la Divinité de Jésus-Christ d'après les Evangiles*, ed. and trans. R. Chidiac, Paris, 1939.

Crusades the bitterness brought about by political events caused the Muslim and Christian communities in the Near East, where their physical contact is closest, to be completely isolated from one another. The same situation is now developing in regard to Judaism as a result of the situation in Palestine. Yet in other parts of the Muslim world where socio-political events did not bring about lasting friction, study of both Christianity and Judaism continued, often with much sympathy, and there have been occasional contacts of a theological and spiritual order between these various communities. Only a century ago the Persian Sufi poet Hâtif Iṣfahânî praised Christianity as being an affirmation of Divine Unity provided its doctrine of trinity is understood in its metaphysical significance. In his memorable poem (*Tarjî' band*) he writes:

In the church I said to a Christian charmer of hearts,
'O thou in whose net the heart is captive!
O thou to the warp of whose girdle each hair-tip
of mine is separately attached!
How long wilt thou continue not to find the way
to the Divine Unity? How long wilt thou impose
on the One the shame of the Trinity?
How can it be right to name the One True God "Father",
"Son", and "Holy Ghost"?'
She parted her sweet lips and said to me, while
with sweet laughter she poured sugar from her lips:
'If thou art aware of the Secret of the Divine Unity,
do not cast on us the stigma of infidelity!
In three mirrors the Eternal Beauty cast a ray
from His effulgent countenance.
Silk does not become three things
if thou callest it *Parniyân*, *Ḥarîr*, and *Parand*.'[15]
While we were thus speaking, this chant
rose up beside us from the church bell:
'He is One and there is naught save He:
There is no God save Him alone!'[16]

During this century the great Algerian Sufi, Shaykh Aḥmad al-'Alawî, echoed this same view when he called for the joining of hands of all religions to combat modern unbelief and showed particular

[15] These are three different words for silk.

[16] Trans. by E. G. Browne in his *A Literary History of Persia*, vol. IV, Cambridge, 1930, pp. 293–4.

interest in Christianity, whose doctrines he knew well.[17] Altogether the contact between Islam and the Judaeo-Christian tradition over the centuries has been immense both on the formal and informal planes. This heritage provides all that is needed for a meaningful encounter between these religions today.

As for the Iranian religions, Islam encountered them also early in its career as it subdued the Sassanid Empire and penetrated into the Iranian plateau. During the three or four centuries when Islam gradually became completely dominant in Persia it had numerous contacts with these religions and especially with Zoroastrianism and Manichaeism. It even influenced some of the later Zoroastrian writings produced in the early Islamic period in the same way that elements of Zoroastrianism were integrated into certain perspectives of Islamic intellectual life.[18] Debates carried on with followers of Iranian religions in Basra and Baghdad itself are recorded in early theological and historical sources. From the beginning the Zoroastrians were accepted as a 'People of the Book' while the Manichaeans were opposed on fundamental theological grounds. Nevertheless the influence of the latter, especially in regard to cosmogonical and cosmological ideas, is to be seen in certain Ismâ'îlî cosmologies and most likely also in some of the writings of Muḥammad ibn Zakariyyâ' al-Râzî. Manichaean beliefs have also been described by many scholars such as Ibn al-Nadîm and Bîrûnî, and in fact Muslim works serve as a valuable source for present-day knowledge of certain aspects of Manichaeism.[19]

Zoroastrianism had more intimate contact with Islam than did Manichaeism. But here again the situation has not been the same in all Muslim lands. Zoroastrianism, although known on the popular level everywhere, was not as much studied in the Arab part of the Muslim world as in Persia which had been its ancient home.[20] In Persia Zoroastrianism provided first of all a vocabulary for Sufi poets like Ḥâfiẓ who often speak of the 'fire-temple', the Zoroastrian priest, etc., as symbols of the Sufi centre (*khâniqâh* or *zâwiyah*), the spiritual

[17] See M. Lings, *A Moslem Saint of the Twentieth Century*, where the Shaykh's interest in other religions is amply treated in the opening chapters.

[18] See W. H. Baily, *Zoroastrian Problems in the Ninth Century Books*, Oxford, 1943.

[19] All the Muslim sources pertaining to Manichaeism are assembled in S. H. Taqizadeh, *Mânî wa dîn-i û*, Tehran, 1335.

[20] Even today many people in the Arab Near East refer to the Hindus as *majûs* or Zoroastrians, not making a distinction on the popular level between the Indian and Iranian traditions.

master, and so on;[21] this manner of speaking, however, does not at all imply an historical influence of Zoroastrianism upon Sufism. Rather is it a means whereby the Sufi asserted the independence of esotericism from the exoteric forms of the revelation, in the sense that esotericism does not derive from exotericism but directly from God who is the source of the revelation containing both dimensions. Zoroastrian angelology and cosmology were also resuscitated by Shihâb al-Dîn Suhrawardî, the founder of the school of Illumination or *Ishrâq*, who made these symbols transparent in the light of Islamic gnosis.[22] In this domain there was also an influence of the *Ishrâqî* school itself upon certain schools of later Zoroastrianism such as the movement connected with the name of Âdhar Kaywân.

It is when we turn to the Indian religions—essentially Hinduism and Buddhism—that from the Islamic point of view the question of understanding and penetrating into religious forms becomes more difficult. This difficulty is brought about not only because of the mythological language of the Indian traditions which is different from the 'abstract' language of Islam, but also because in going from the one tradition to the others one moves from the background of the Abrahamic traditions to a different spiritual climate. Nevertheless Islam has had profound contact with the religions of India on both the formal and metaphysical planes. Already through the Indian sciences which had reached the Muslims both through Pahlavi and directly from Sanskrit, some knowledge had been gained of Indian culture during the early Islamic period. But it is thanks to the incomparable *Taḥqîq mâ li'l-hind* or *India* of Bîrûnî, a work unique in the exactitude of its compilation, that medieval Muslims gained a knowledge of Hinduism, especially the Vishnavite school with which Bîrûnî seems to have been best acquainted.[23] He was also responsible

[21] The symbolism of Ḥâfiẓ's delicate and exquisite language has never been fully expounded in any Western language. One of the best translations and commentaries upon him is *The Dîvân, Written in the Fourteenth Century by Khwâja Shamsu-d-Dîn Muḥammad-i-Ḥâfiẓ-i Shîrâzî otherwise known as Lisânu-l-Ghaib and Tarjumânu-l-Asrâr* by Lieut.-Col. H. Wilberforce Clarke, Calcutta, 2 vols., 1891.

[22] See S. H. Nasr, *Three Muslim Sages* chapter II; also S. H. Nasr, 'Suhrawardî' in *A History of Muslim Philosophy*. See also the many studies of H. Corbin on Suhrawardî, especially *Opera Metaphysica et Mystica*, vol. II, Tehran, 1952, prolegomena and *Les motifs zoroastriens dans la philosophie de Sohrawardî*, Tehran, 1946-1325.

[23] For a summary of Bîrûnî's views on Hinduism see A. Jeffery, 'Al-Biruni's Contribution to Comparative Religion', in *Al-Bîrûnî Commemoration Volume*, Calcutta, 1951, pp. 125–60; also S. H. Nasr, *An Introduction to Islamic Cosmological Doctrines*, Chapter V.

for the translation of the *Patañjali Yoga* into Arabic, and in fact inaugurated a tradition of contact with Hinduism which, although interrupted by several gaps in time, continued through Amîr Khusraw Dihlawî, to Abu'l-Faḍl, Dârâ Shukûh, and the vast movement of translation of Hindu works into Persian in the Moghul period.[24]

On the religious plane, although the Zoroastrians were definitely included among the *ahl al-kitâb* or 'people of the Book', there was a debate among the general Muslim public as to where Hinduism stood, although as already mentioned many of the *'ulamâ'* of India definitely considered Hindus as 'people of the Book'. It goes without saying that in India itself the Muslims certainly did not treat the Hindus as simple pagans or idol-worshippers like those of Arabia but came to respect them as possessing a religion of their own. As already mentioned, many Sufis in India called Hinduism the religion of Adam, and such an orthodox Naqshbandî saint as Mirzâ Maẓhar Jân Jânân considered the Vedas as divinely inspired. There was, in fact, in Islam a presentiment of the primordial character of Hinduism which moved many Muslim authors to identify Brahman with Abraham. This connection may seem strange linguistically but it contains a deep metaphysical significance. Abraham is, for Islam, the original patriarch identified with the primordial religion (*al-dîn al-ḥanîf*) which Islam came to reassert and reaffirm. The connection of the name of the *barâhimah* (namely Hindus) with Abraham was precisely an assertion of the primordial nature of the Hindu tradition in the Muslim mind.

The Sufi master 'Abd al-Karîm al-Jîlî writes in his *al-Insân al-kâmil:*

'The people of the book are divided into many groups. As for the *barâhimah* [Hindus] they claim that they belong to the religion of Abraham and that they are of his progeny and possess special acts of worship. . . . The *barâhimah* worship God absolutely without [recourse to] prophet or messenger. In fact, they say there is nothing in the world of existence except that it be the created of God. They testify to His Oneness in Being, but deny the prophets and messengers completely. Their worship of the Truth is like that of the prophets

[24] For two different views of the interaction between Islam and Hinduism in India see Tara Chand, *The Influence of Islam on Indian Culture*, Allahabad, 1954, and A. Ahmad, *Studies in Islamic Culture in its Indian Environment*, Oxford, 1964, which also contains a rich bibliography on the subject.

before their prophetic mission. They claim to be the children of Abraham—upon whom be peace—and say that they possess a book written for them by Abraham—upon whom be peace—himself, except that they say that it came from His Lord. In it the truth of things is mentioned and it has five parts. As for the four parts they permit their reading to everyone. But as for the fifth part they do not allow its reading except to a few among them, because of its depth and unfathomableness. It is well known among them that whoever reads the fifth part of their book will of necessity come into the fold of Islam and enter into the religion of Muḥammad—upon whom be peace.'[25]

Al-Jîlî distinguishes between Hindu metaphysics and the daily practice of the Hindus and identifies especially their metaphysical doctrines with the doctrine of Divine Unity in Islam. His reference to the 'Fifth Veda' signifies precisely the inner identity of the esoteric and metaphysical doctrines of the two traditions. He, like the other Sufis, sought to approach Hinduism through a metaphysical penetration into its mythological structure to reveal the presence of the One behind the veil of the many. In this domain his approach was not basically different from the attitude of those Sufis who tried to interpret the Christian Trinity as an assertion rather than a negation of Divine Unity.

The translation of Hindu works into Persian during the Moghul period is an event of great spiritual significance whose full import has not as yet been explored, especially by non-Persian and non-Indian Muslims. The central figure in this movement was the prince Dârâ Shukûh who was responsible for the translation of the *Bhagavad-Gîtâ*, the *Yoga Vasishtha*, and, most important of all, the *Upanishads*. It was from his Persian version that the Latin translation of Anquetil-Duperron was made, a translation which influenced many

[25] *Al-Insân al-kâmil*, Cairo, 1304, II, pp. 78 and 87. Of course many authors of works on religious sects denied this connection, like al-Shahristânî, who writes: 'There are those among the people who believe they [the Hindus] are called *Barâhimah* because of their affiliation to Abraham—upon whom be peace. But this is wrong, for they are a people especially known to have denied prophecy completely and totally.' *al-Milal wa'l-niḥal*, Cairo, 1347, IV, p. 135. Needless to say this theological criticism does not in any way detract from the metaphysical significance of the assertion of al-Jîlî.

Regarding the relation between Hinduism and Islam as the first and last traditions of this human cycle see R. Guénon, 'The Mysteries of the Letter Nûn', in *Art and Thought*, ed. K. B. Iyer, London, 1947, pp. 166–8; also the series of articles by M. Valsân entitled, 'Le Triangle de l'Androgyne et le monosyllabe "Om" ', in *Etudes traditionnelles* of 1964 and 1965.

of the nineteenth-century European philosophers like Schelling and a copy of which was owned by the mystic poet William Blake.[26]

Whatever the significance of this translation has been for the spread of Hindu studies in the West, it is even more significant for the question of the religious encounter between Hinduism and Islam today. In the same way that the Crusades nearly destroyed amicable contacts between Islam and Christianity in the Near East, the events of the past century have embittered the contact between Hinduism and Islam in the Indian sub-continent itself, and perhaps a land like Persia, where there has been both the historical contact with Hinduism and lack of bitter political encounters during recent times, could be a more suitable place for making a basic study of the relations between Hinduism and Islam on the highest level.

Be that as it may, the translations of Dârâ Shukûh do not at all indicate a syncretism or eclecticism as one finds in certain other mixed movements in India. Dârâ was a Sufi of the Qâdiriyyah order and a devout Muslim. He believed the *Upanishads* to be the 'Hidden Books' to which the Quran refers (lvi. 77–80) and wrote that: 'They contain the essence of unity and they are secrets which have to be kept hidden!'[27] His *Majma' al-baḥrayn* is an attempt to show the identity of the Muslim and Hindu doctrines of unity. It is enough to read Dârâ Shukûh's translation of any of the *Upanishads* to realize that he was not only translating words into Persian but also ideas into the framework of Sufism. His translations contain a Sufi view of the *Upanishads* and, far from being an attempt to syncretize, represent a serious effort to create a bridge between Hindu and Islamic metaphysics. His translations and numerous others of such Hindu classics as the *Râmâyaṇa*, the *Mahâbhârata* and the *Yoga Vasíshtha*, upon which the Persian sage Mîr Abu'l-Qâsim Findiriskî wrote a commentary, are a veritable treasure which should become known to the Muslim world at large and not remain confined to the Persians and

[26] The Persian text of the *Upanishads* has been edited in a modern edition by Tara Chand and J. Nâ'înî as *Sirr-i akbar*, Tehran, 1957-60. See the English introduction of Tara Chand concerning Dârâ Shukûh's writings and their significance. The Persian translations of Dârâ Shukûh were also important for the preservation of Hindu doctrines for the Hindus themselves in the eighteenth and nineteenth century so that a nineteenth-century Hindu translator of the *Upanishads* refers to Dârâ Shukûh as one of the revivers of Hinduism along with Shankarâ-charyâ and Vyasa. See M. H. Askari, 'Tradition et modernisme. . . .', p. 120.

[27] *Ibid.*, p. 45 of Tara Chand's introduction.

the Muslims of the Indo-Pakistani sub-continent.[28] These writings, as well as those of other Sufi masters in Muslim India such as Ghawth 'Alî Shâh, the Sufi expositor of Tantrism, and many others, who have often given the most penetrating explanations of Hindu metaphysics and mythology, can serve as a basis for a serious study of the Hindu tradition in the light of modern conditions.

It is surprising that although Islam had so much contact with Buddhism there is much less about this tradition in Muslim sources than about Hinduism. Of course, through the translation of the *Pancha Tântra* into Arabic from Pahlavi as well as through other literary sources and oral traditions, something was known of the personality of the Buddha as a wise man, and he was often identified with the figure of Hermes as the origin of wisdom.[29] Many of the common sources of religious schools and sects considered Buddhism as a branch of Hinduism,[30] and even Bîrûnî in his *India* devoted little attention to it.

The most serious and noteworthy study of Buddhism in Islamic annals outside the works written more recently by Indian Muslims comes rather late, in the eighth/fourteenth century, in the universal history of Rashîd al-Dîn Faḍlallâh.[31] The chapter devoted to Buddhism, a religion which must have attracted new attention with the coming of the Mongols, is based mostly upon collections of traditions and the direct assistance of a Kashmiri lama named Kâmalashrî-Bakhshî. The chapter includes an account of Indian mythology drawn mostly from the *Purâṇas* and the best Muslim description of the Yuga cycles, but all seen from the Buddhist rather than the Hindu point of view. The most outstanding aspect of the work, however, is the account of the life of the Buddha,[32] which is unique in Islamic writings. He is considered a prophet with a book called *Abi dharma* containing the quintessence of truth. As is to be expected, the Muslims

[28] The profound comparative study of the *Yoga Vasishtha* by Mîr Findiriskî is a highlight of Hindu-Muslim metaphysical studies perhaps even surpassing in depth the works of Dârâ Shukûh. A study is currently being made of this work by the Persian scholar, Fatḥallâh Mujtabâ'î.

[29] See S. H. Nasr, *Islamic Studies* chapter IV.

[30] Al-Shahristânî divides the Hindus into three groups, one of whom he calls *aṣḥâb al-budadah* or Buddhists. He says that the first *budd* was called *shâkin* (Shakyamuni) and below him stands the rank of *al-bardî sa'îyah* (?) most likely meaning the Boddhisattiva. He also gives some account of Buddhist asceticism and moral teachings. *Op. cit.*, pp. 139 ff.

[31] See K. Jahn, 'On the mythology and religion of the Indians in the medieval Moslem tradition', in *Mélanges Henri Massé* pp. 185–97.

[32] See K. Jahn, 'Kâmalashrî-Rashîd al-Dîn's "Life and teaching of the Buddha"', *Central Asiatic Journal*, vol. II, 1956, pp. 81–128.

see all 'divine descents' or *Avatâras* as prophets in the Islamic sense, so that such a treatment of the Buddha should not be in any way surprising. This valuable account of the life of Shakyamuni became well known and was incorporated in several later Persian works on universal history. But there was no further work of any great significance in this field as there was in the case of Hinduism, mostly because the same opportunity of direct contact with Buddhism did not present itself later save in western China, where the Muslim community continued to live relatively isolated from the main stream of Islamic intellectual life.

III

This analysis of some of the features of the historical contact between Islam and other religions has revealed the fact that during its history Islam has felt the presence of other traditions on different levels, and in different modes, which may be enumerated as essentially: the *Sharî ah*; theology; history; science, philosophy, and learning; and finally Sufism or esotericism. On each level the encounter with other religions has had a meaning and continues to do so and each encounter can contribute to the total understanding of other traditions.

On the level of the *Sharî'ah* Islam has always seen other religions as a Divine Law like itself. Many medieval jurists referred to the *shar'* of other prophets and peoples, and Islamic Law itself gives freedom within the Islamic world (*dâr al-islâm*) for other people having their own Divine Law to follow their own ways within their community, wherein they enjoy complete religious independence. Many studies have been made of what one might call 'comparative religious law' in which the religious injunctions of different communities have been described and compared. The Muslim jurists were also the first to develop the science of international law, of trying to provide means whereby relations between peoples following differing codes of law could be established. This description and morphological study of the sacred laws of other religions is one that can in fact be pursued today on the basis established by the classical jurists.

Theological debates occurred early between Muslims and followers of other faiths, incited especially by the Mu'tazilites who were interested in this subject. Also discussions about different religions were held with some of the Shi'ite Imâms and often by adherents of these religions themselves, as is recorded in Shi'ite sources such as Ibn Bâbûyah. Likewise, Ismâ'îlî authors continued to interest themselves in other religions particularly because of their emphasis upon the cycles of prophecy and the universality of esotericism.[33] There grew from these theological debates the numerous works on 'sects' or *al-Milal wa'l-niḥal*, to the extent that one can say that the Muslims were the founders of the science of comparative religion. Many outstanding theologians—Shi'ites and Sunnis alike—wrote works of this kind like *Kitâb al-maqâlât wa'l-firaq* of Sa'd ibn 'Abdallâh al-Ash'arî al-Qumî, the *Kitâb firaq al-shî'ah* of al-Nawbakhtî, the *Farq bayn al-firaq* of al-Baghdâdî, the *Maqâlât al-islâmiyyîn* of Abu'l-Ḥasan al-Ash'arî, the founder of Ash'arite theology,[34] *al-Faṣl* of Ibn Ḥazm, *I'tiqâdât firaq al-muslimîn* of Fakhr al-Dîn al-Râzî, and the best-known work of this kind, *al-Milal wa'l-niḥal* of al-Shahristânî. All of these authors were outstanding theologians and their approach is primarily theological and usually polemical. But inasmuch as again in modern times theological debates have come to take place, especially between Christianity, Judaism and Islam, these works can serve as a basis and provide a background for the task that lies ahead in this domain.

Then there is the tradition of historians who tried to describe simply in as objective a manner as possible what they saw or read of other religions and religious cultures. We see such an approach in the writings of universal historians like al-Mas'ûdî and al-Ya'qûbî. Al-Mas'ûdî also wrote a special treatise on religions, entitled *al-Maqâlât fî uṣûl al-diyânât*. There are the *Fihrist* of Ibn al-Nadîm and the *Bayân al-adyân* of Abu'l-Ma'âlî Muḥammad ibn 'Ubaydallâh, where

[33] See, for example, the *Kashf al-maḥjûb* of Abû Ya'qûb Sijistânî, ed. H. Corbin, Jāmil'al Tehran, 1949, pp. 77–9, on the necessity of the plurality of prophets and religions because of changing conditions of the people to whom revelation is addressed. The author adds that each prophet reveals an aspect of the truth and the Divine Law so that it is necessary to have many prophets to reveal the different aspects of truth and also reaffirm what came before in the way of revelation.

Likewise Nâṣir-i Khusraw in his *Jāmil' al-ḥikmatayn*, ed. H. Corbin and M. Mo'in, Tehran, 1953, speaks of Christ as the 'Word of God' and of the universality of the prophetic chain before the Prophet of Islam. The universality of revelation is a permanent theme of both Twelve-Imâm Shi'ite and Ismâ'ïlî theology as it is with Sufism in general, although the standpoint remains within the bounds of the Abrahamic tradition.

[34] This important work edited by H. Ritter as *Die dogmatischen Lehren der Anhanger des Islam*, Wiesbaden, 1963, as well as al-Ash'arî's *Maqâlât al-mulḥidîn*, which is its complementary volume dealing more directly with non-Islamic groups and sects, reveals how much interest the study of religions held for even those Muslim theologians who tried to oppose rationalistic discourse on religion and were the defenders of the letter of the revelation.

Some theologians dealt even in their theological works, with the history of religions, which they treated in a separate section; al-Îjî in his *al-Mawâqif* provides an example.

a very fair account of religions is given, and there are references by both Bîrûnî and Nâşir-i Khusraw to Abu'l-'Abbas Îrân-shahrî, who is said to have studied the doctrines of other religions with genuine interest. There is the incomparable Bîrûnî himself who, not only in his *India* but also in the *Chronology of Ancient Nations* and many other works, has provided a wealth of information about so many different religions. This tradition continued in later universal histories up to very recent times in such works as the *Nâsikh al-tawârîkh* which was compiled in Persia only about a century ago. But these later works were mostly repetitions of earlier ones when it came to religious matters. This tradition of objective accounts of other religions could again serve as a basis for contemporary works in Muslim languages on Hinduism, Buddhism, Shintoism, and even the religions of the American Indians, as well as on Christianity and Judaism; however many such works in Islamic languages have been compiled by non-Muslim authors for reasons other than that of creating understanding between religions. Such descriptive accounts should be based upon genuine sources; and especially as far as the Oriental traditions are concerned, they should not be an echo of the mistakes and prejudices of Western works translated into Arabic, Persian, Turkish, etc., as is in fact often the case.[35]

In the sphere of science and philosophy and learning in general the integration of elements from these fields into the Islamic world-view meant also contact with the religion of the civilizations from which the material in question came. It must be remembered that in a traditional civilization every science is connected in one way or another with the religious principles of that civilization. The Indian medicine and astronomy that the Muslims soon absorbed also brought them

[35] The very commendable work of Kenneth Morgan and a few others in America and England should here be mentioned, their aim being to provide means of learning about religions based on the writings of those who believe in them and live within their world view; this method of approaching the subject could also be adopted by Muslims with advantage. If Muslims want to know about Christianity it is best to seek this knowledge from a Christian who believes in it, not one who has 'outgrown' it in his own mind. And for even stronger reasons they should want to hear from a Buddhist about Buddhism or a Hindu about Hinduism or to learn of these religions from the very few Western authors who have either themselves had direct contact with these traditions or are particularly endowed both through inner sympathy and innate intelligence to understand the forms and symbols of other religions than their own. The large number of second-hand works on comparative religion now being translated from European languages into Arabic, Persian, etc., calls for a definite Muslim answer before, in yet another field of study, the minds of modern educated Muslims become fatally contaminated. Until now only a few works based on genuine sources have appeared, but they are far too few to answer the need for such literature today.

into contact with certain Hindu cosmological ideas. Indian and Persian works on natural history acquainted Muslims with the religious conception of nature present in these works. As for the Graeco-Hellenistic sciences, although the Muslims were not interested in the Olympic pantheon, through Greek philosophical and scientific works they came to learn of the Orphic-Pythagorean element of the Greek tradition, which interested them immensely, precisely because it was an assertion of the doctrine of Divine Unity. If they called Plato the *imâm* of the philosophers and Plotinus 'the Shaykh of the Greeks' (namely, their Sufi master) it was again because in their writings they saw the expression of that metaphysical doctrine that Islam was to expound later. In the *Ishrâqî* theosophy of Suhrawardî, moreover, there is continuous reference to the universality of a wisdom which was shared by all nations of old and which found its universal expression in Islamic gnosis.[36] It is that wisdom which Steuben, Leibniz and the Neoscholastics were later to call the *philosophia perennis*, an expression to which A. K. Coomaraswamy quite rightly added the epithet *et universalis*.

It is, however, on the level of esotericism, in the perspective of Sufism, that the most profound encounter with other traditions has been made and where one can find the indispensable ground for the understanding in depth of other religions today. The Sufi is one who seeks to transcend the world of forms, to journey from multiplicity to Unity, from the particular to the Universal. He leaves the many for the One and through this very process is granted the vision of the One in the many. For him all forms become transparent, including religious forms, thus revealing to him their unique origin. Sufism or Islamic gnosis is the most universal affirmation of that perennial wisdom which stands at the heart of Islam and in fact of all religion as such.[37] It is this supreme doctrine of Unity—which is itself unique

[36] The figure of Hermes invoked by Suhrawardî and many other Muslim sages as the bringer of a revelation which was the origin of all philosophy or rather theosophy, signifies belief in the universality of wisdom, the *religio perennis*.

For the importance of the figure of Hermes as the symbol of a primordial religion see M. Eliade, 'The Quest for the "Origins of Religion"', pp. 154–6. However, it is of great significance that the Hermetic movement in the Renaissance was essentially against the all-embracing medieval Christian tradition, whereas in Islam the figure of Hermes fitted perfectly well into Islamic prophetology.

[37] It is this gnosis which stands as the best proof of the truth of religion as such because the gnostic sees religion as an inseparable aspect of human existence. There is no better proof of the existence of God than man, who confirms his creator through his theomorphic nature and particularly through his intelligence which stands as the proof of the Absolute that is its real object.

'Human nature in general and human intelligence in particular cannot be (*al-tawḥîd wâḥid*)—that the Sufis call the 'religion of love' and to which Ibn 'Arabî refers in his well-known verses in the *Tarjumân al-ashwâq*.[38] This love is not merely sentiment or emotions, it is the realized aspect of gnosis. It is a transcendent knowledge that reveals the inner unity of religions. Shabistarî in his *Gulshan-i râz* refers to this very truth when he says:

> Necessary Being is as Heaven and Hell as contingent,
> 'I' and 'You' are the Hades veil between them.
> When this veil is lifted up from before you,
> There remains not the bond of sects and creeds.
> All the authority of the law is over this 'I' of yours,
> Since that is bound to your soul and body,
> When 'I' and 'You' remain not in the midst,
> What is mosque, what is synagogue, what is fire temple?[39]

Although not all Sufis have dealt specifically with the question of other traditions, some have gone into detailed discussion of this matter. Ibn 'Arabî, one of the Sufis whose vocation it was to expound

understood apart from the phenomenon of religion, which characterizes them in the most direct and most complete way possible. If we can grasp the transcendent nature (not the "psychological" nature) of the human being, we thereby grasp the nature of revelation, of religion, of tradition; we understand their possibility, their necessity, their truth. And in understanding religion, not only in a particular form or according to some verbal specification, but also in its formless essence, we understand the religions, that is to say, the meaning of their plurality and their diversity; this is the plane of gnosis, of the *religio perennis*, whereon the extrinsic antimonies of dogma are explained and resolved.' F. Schuon, '*Religio Perennis*', in *Light on the Ancient Worlds*, p. 142.

38
> My heart has become capable of every form: it is
> a pasture for gazelles and a convent for Christians
> And a temple for idols and the pilgrim's Ka'ba and
> the tables of the Torah, and the book of the Koran.
> I follow the religion of Love: whatever way Love's camels
> take, that is my religion and my faith.

Tarjumân al-ashwâq, trans. by R. A. Nicholson, London, 1911, p. 67; see also S. H. Nasr, *Three Muslim Sages*, pp. 116–18.

It need hardly be pointed out that this vision of the transcendent unity of religions stands at the very antipodes of the modern syncretisms and pseudo-spiritualities which have been growing during the past few decades as a result of the weakening of tradition in the West. Not only do they not succeed in transcending forms but they fall beneath them, opening the door to all kinds of evil forces affecting those who are unfortunate enough to be duped by their so-called universalism.

39 *Gulshan-i râz*, p. 31.

the doctrines of Sufism in their fullness, asserts openly the doctrine of the universality of revelation. He writes:

'Know that when God, the Exalted, created the creatures He created them in kinds and in each kind He placed the best and chose from the best the élite. These are the faithful (*mu'minûn*). And He chose from the faithful the élite, who are the saints, and from these élite the quintessence. These are the prophets (*anbiyâ'*). And from this quintessence He chose the finest parts and they are the prophets who bring a Divine Law. . . .'[40]

Ibn 'Arabî and al-Jîlî after him also elaborated the doctrine of the Logos according to which the founder of each religion is an aspect of the universal logos, which they identify with the 'Reality of Muḥammad' (*al-ḥaqîqat al-muḥammadiyyah*).[41] The masterpiece of Ibn 'Arabî, the *Fuṣûṣ al-ḥikam*, or *Bezels of Wisdom*, is in fact an exposition of the particular spiritual genuis of each prophet as 'a Word of God'. Moreover, the Sufis believe that in the same way that each being in the Universe is the theophany (*tajallî*) of a Divine Name, so does each religion reveal an aspect of the Divine Names and Qualities. The multiplicity of religions is a direct result of the infinite richness of the Divine Being. Al-Jîlî writes:

'There is nothing in existence except that it worships God the Most High in its state and speech and acts, nay in its essence and qualities. And everything in existence obeys God Most High. But acts of worship differ because of the difference of the exigencies of the Divine Names and Qualities.'[42]

The Sufis not only assert the unity of revelation but also consider themselves as the guardians of Islam and, moreover, of all traditions. To quote al-Jîlî once again,

'The [gnostics] are the investigators of the truth upon whom God has constructed the foundations of existence. The spheres of the worlds

[40] *Al-Futûḥât al-makkiyyah*, Cairo, 1293, vol. II, pp. 73–74.

[41] This fundamental doctrine expounded mostly in the *Fuṣûṣ* of Ibn 'Arabî and the *Al-Insân al-kâmil* of al-Jîlî has been explained with remarkable clarity in the introduction and notes of the masterly translations of these works by T. Burckhardt, *La Sagesse des prophètes* and *De l'homme universel*.

The doctrine of the Logos according to Ibn 'Arabî is also summarized in his *Shajarat al-kawn*. See the translation of it by A. Jeffery in *Studia Islamica*, vol. X, pp. 43–77, and vol. XI, pp. 113–60. His notes and explanations, however, do not at all accord with the Islamic view.

[42] *Al-Insân al-kâmil*, II, pp. 76–7.

rotate about them. They are the centre of God's attention in the world, nay, the centre of God's [theophany] in existence. . . . God has erected the foundation of religion, nay, the foundation of all religions upon the ground of their gnosis.'[43]

The Sufis have lived throughout Islamic history with a consciousness of the universality of the wisdom whose means of attainment they bear within their doctrines and methods. But some have had the special vocation to speak explicitly on this matter while others have remained silent. Jalâl al-Dîn Rûmî, who even had some Christian and Jewish disciples and whose *Mathnawî* is replete with verses asserting the universality of tradition, writes in his *Fîhi mâ fîhi*, or *Discourses*, with direct allusion to different traditions:

'I was speaking one day amongst a group of people, and a party of non-Muslims were present. In the middle of my address they began to weep and to register emotion and ecstacy.

'Someone asked: What do they understand and what do they know? Only one Muslim in a thousand understands this kind of talk. What did they understand, that they should weep?

'The Master answered: It is not necessary that they should understand the inner spirit of these words. The root of the matter is the words themselves, and that they do understand. After all, every one acknowledges the Oneness of God, that He is the Creator and Provider, that He controls everything, that to Him all things shall return, and that it is He who punishes and forgives. When anyone hears these words, which are a description and commemoration of God, a universal commotion and ecstatic passion supervenes, since out of these words comes the scent of their Beloved and their Quest.

'Though the ways are various, the goal is one. Do you not see that there are many roads to the Kaaba? For some the road is from Rum, for some from Syria, for some from Persia, for some from China, for some by sea from India and Yemen. So if you consider the roads, the variety is great and the divergence infinite; but when you consider the goal, they are all of one accord and one. The hearts of all are at one upon the Kaaba. The hearts have one attachment, an ardour and a great love for the Kaaba, and in that there is no room for contrariety. That attachment is neither infidelity nor faith; that is to say, that attachment is not confounded with the various roads which we

[43] *Ibid.*, p. 83.

In fact has not this assertion of this great medieval Sufi been realized during this century by those who have sought to defend all traditions against forces that threaten not only a particular religion but religion itself?

have mentioned. Once they have arrived there, that disputation and war and diversity touching the roads—this man saying to that man, "You are false, you are an infidel", and the other replying in kind—once they have arrived at the Kaaba, it is realized that the warfare was concerning the roads only, that their goal was one. . . .

'To resume: now all men in their inmost hearts love God and seek Him, pray to Him and in all things put their hope in Him, recognizing none but Him as omnipotent and ordering their affairs. Such an apperception is neither infidelity nor faith. Inwardly it has no name. . . .

'Now the literalists take the Holy Mosque to be that Kaaba to which people repair. Lovers, however, and the elect of God, take the Holy Mosque to mean union with God. . . .'

Continuing to expound the meaning of this union above the world of forms, he adds:

'If I were to occupy myself with expounding that subtlely, even the saints who have attained God would lose the thread of discourse. How then is it possible to speak of such mysteries and mystic states to mortal men? . . . One man does not see a camel on the top of a minaret; how then shall he see the thread of a hair in the mouth of the camel?'[44]

Not everyone may be able to see the camel on the top of the minaret, much less to distinguish the hair in its mouth. But those who are possessed of such a vision are bound by duty to explain to others to the greatest extent possible what they have seen. Scholarship today can do much in bringing to life unedited texts and making known many chapters in the history of contact between Islam and other religions that have been forgotten. But it remains for the Sufis to expound the metaphysical background in the light of which particular forms can be studied and understood. That is not to say that only the perfect saint, the *wâṣil* (one who has reached the goal), can speak of the inner unity of religions. Only such a person can speak from realized and lived experience. But others who are endowed with intellectual intuition can anticipate intellectually the Centre where all the radii meet, the summit which all roads reach. Only such a vision of the Centre can provide a meaningful dialogue between religions, showing both their inner unity and formal diversity which itself contributes to the richness of modern man's spiritual life and which

[44] *Discourses of Rûmî*, trans. by A. J. Arberry, London, 1961, pp. 108–12. One must be grateful to Professor Arberry for making available to the outside world this rather remarkable work of Rûmî which reveals an aspect of Sufism not often found in more formal Sufi texts.

is given as a compensation for the spiritually starved environment in which he lives.

As far as Islam is concerned the key necessary for opening the door towards a true encounter with other religions has already been provided by Sufism. It is for contemporary Muslims to use this key and to apply the established principles to the particular condition presented to the Islamic world today. It is only through the possession of a metaphysical doctrine of distinguishing between the true and the false, grounded in traditional orthodoxy, that so many pitfalls which exist in the way of a serious study of religions can be averted. And it is only through such a doctrine that a firm basis can be established for a more formal encounter with other religions on the theological and social planes.

He who has gained a vision of that mountain top that touches the Infinite rests assured that climbers who are following other paths are nevertheless his companions on this journey which is the only meaningful journey of life itself. His certainty comes not only from the vision of the peak but also from his knowledge that those paths that have been chosen for man by God Himself do ultimately lead to the top whatever turns they may make on the way. As far as Islam is concerned this knowledge is already contained within the treasure-house of Islamic wisdom. It is for contemporary Muslims to seek this wisdom, to make it their own and then to make use of it in conformity with their real needs.

X

The Ecological Problem in the Light of Sufism: The Conquest of Nature and the Teachings of Eastern Science

In a sense the problem of the presence of other religions and of the presence of Nature are related from the point of view of the most current trends in Christian theology, for in these theological perspectives both problems concern realities cut off from the grace of the Christian revelation. It is no accident that K. Barth and his followers are so adamantly opposed or at least indifferent to both a 'theology of comparative religion' and a 'theology of nature'. To extend the horizons of man to embrace other forms of revelation should include nature as well, since from the metaphysical point of view this also is a revelation of God, conveying its own spiritual message and possessing its own spiritual methods.[1] Strangely enough modern man is faced with both of these problems at the same time. He is in desperate need of gaining a new vision of nature and of his own relation with it in order to survive even physically; likewise he needs to reach a more profound understanding of other religions in order to better understand himself, not to speak of becoming better acquainted with segments of humanity other than his own.

In Islam the key necessary for the solution of both problems is to be found in Sufism. In the previous chapter our task was to apply Sufism's teachings to the problem posed for Islam by the presence of other religions. In the present essay these same teachings have to be applied to the question of the conquest of nature, which has taken on a most urgent character in the West and also in Japan, but which for the moment at least has not succeeded in attracting the attention of most

[1] 'Utterly untouched nature has of itself the character of a sanctuary and this it is considered to be by most nomadic and semi-nomadic peoples, particularly the Red Indians. . . . For Hindus the forest is the natural dwelling-place of sages and we meet with a similar valuation of the sacred aspect of nature in all traditions which have, even indirectly, a primordial and mythological character.' F. Schuon, *Spiritual Perspectives and Human Facts*, p. 46.

of the Muslim intelligentsia, although in their case also it is bound to become a crucial question soon.[2] In examining this problem it has seemed expedient to deal with the Eastern sciences in general rather than with Islamic science alone, seeing that in the question of the relation of man to nature there is a profound harmony among these sciences,[3] and also in view of the fact that the question of the relation of man and nature and the crisis brought about in this realm by modern civilization has world-wide repercussions.

It is interesting to note how the cry of a few seers in the wilderness just a generation ago has today become the battle-cry of so many men who are intelligent enough to perceive the catastrophic effects that the further pursuit of the ways followed by Western civilization in its treatment of nature during the past four or five centuries can have for all humanity. If a few lonely voices in past years warned of the dangers that would follow in the path of indefinite material expansion and so-called 'development' or 'progress', today a great many people realize that the goal of the 'conquest of nature', which has seemed the most obvious aim of modern civilization, can no longer be pursued. The very success of modern man in conquering nature has itself become a major danger. All the problems caused by the unilateral attitude of modern man towards nature, from over-population and mass pollution to the lowering of the quality of human life itself and the threat of its actual destruction, have at least caused those capable of reflection to pause a moment and to examine the assumptions upon which modern science and its applications are based. Somehow, something has gone wrong in the application of a science that purports to be an objective knowledge of nature shorn from all spiritual and metaphysical considerations. The application of such a science seems to aid in destroying its very object. Nature seems to cry out that the knowledge derived from it through the techniques of modern Western science and then applied to it once

[2] It is unfortunately one of the worst characteristics of this age that people wait until they fall into a pitfall and only then begin to struggle to climb out of it. When one mentions the immediacy of the ecological problem and the necessity to have greater foresight in industrial and enconomic planning to most modernized Muslims, especially those responsible for carrying out such programmes, the stereotyped answer is that we should wait until we reach the economic level of the West and then think about such problems, to which one could simply answer that by that time it will be too late to do anything effective.

[3] We have dealt more extensively with this problem in *The Encounter of Man and Nature: the Spiritual Crisis of Modern Man.*

As for the Sufi conception of nature see Nasr, *Science and Civilization in Islam*, chapter 13; Nasr, *Islamic Studies*, chapter 13; and T. Burckhardt, *Clé spirituelle de l'astrologie musulmane*, Paris, 1950.

again through technology leaves aside a whole aspect of its reality, without which it could not continue to survive as the complete and harmonious whole that in fact it is. Considering the gravity of the situation, it is to this crucial problem, to the limitations of Western science and its unending applications with the aim of 'conquering nature', that we must now address ourselves by drawing from the sapiential teachings of the Oriental traditions or of what in this essay we can call 'Eastern science'.[4]

Before everything else it is essential to clarify what is meant by Eastern science. For our purpose here it means the sciences of the great traditions of Asia, especially the Chinese and Japanese, the Indian and the Islamic. By extension, this term could embrace other traditional sciences, but it is sufficient here to limit ourselves to the cases cited above. Although far from being identical in themselves, these sciences share a fundamental principle in common, which is to regard the sciences of nature in the light of metaphysical principles, or from another point of view, to study nature as a domain that is 'contained and embraced' by a supra-sensible world that is immensely greater than it. Because of this basic principle and many other features that are directly or indirectly related to it, one can definitely speak of Eastern science as a body of knowledge containing a distinct vision of things in contrast to Western science as it has developed since the Renaissance and as it has spread to other continents during the present century.

Moreover, in this essay the term 'science' will be deliberately used rather than, let us say, 'philosophy' or 'religion', precisely because in the present discussion one is envisaging a science of nature which is akin in subject matter if not in method and point of view to 'science' as currently understood in Western parlance. For decades people have contrasted Eastern spirituality in such forms as Sufism and the Vedanta with Western science and have written of how each has been successful and borne fruit in its own way. It has been said more than once, especially by modern orientals, that the East must learn science from the West and that the West does not have to learn geology or botany from the East but, as even some Westerners have conceded, can profit from an acquaintance with eastern religion and spirituality. We can be the first to agree that the West needs to learn metaphysics

[4] Although there are, of course, many different schools of science in each of the Oriental traditions, they are close enough in their teachings concerning the spiritual significance of nature and the relation of man to it to allow of one's using this term; there is no question here of overlooking the diversity within the Oriental traditions themselves.

and traditional sapiential doctrines from the East if it is to preserve and revive anything at all of its own spiritual heritage. This is a dazzlingly evident reality which any profound study of comparative religion and of the present state of mentality in the West would reveal. Many have journeyed to the lands of the East, especially those lands which have preserved to this day their spiritual heritage, such as Japan, India and the Islamic world, for just this reason.

Fewer people realize, however, that even on the level of the sciences of nature the East has something extremely precious to offer to the modern world. Just to cite a few examples, Islamic natural philosophy and physics, or Indian alchemy, or Chinese and Japanese medicine, or even, one might add, geomancy—whose practice, known as *Fung Shui*, is still prevalent in China—have something to say about the situation that the application of modern science has brought about in the form of the ecological crisis everyone now fears so greatly.

The Eastern sciences, which must be made more accessible and better known by the few historians of science specializing in these fields, were successful through just what appears in modern eyes as their failure. Modern science on the other hand is in a sense facing failure—especially through its alliance with technology and the spirit of conquest over nature—because of its very success. In this major dilemma the modern world needs not only Eastern spirituality and metaphysics, which evidently are the essence and fundamental basis of all the Eastern traditions and contain the principles of all the traditional sciences, but also the curative influence of the world view contained in the Eastern sciences of nature.

Hitherto, the educated reader found it well nigh impossible to take seriously the world view of the Eastern sciences and this still is the case in most Western 'intellectual' circles. Western science has 'advanced', in whatever sense we define this ambiguous term, by negating all other possible sciences of nature. Its monolithic and monopolistic character has been part and parcel of its image of its own self, although there is no logic whatsoever which would deny the possibility of other legitimate forms of science existing alongside it. The sense of pride that has accompanied the particular type of mental activity called 'modern science' is such that it relegates anything that does not conform to its view of what true science should be to the realm of 'pseudo-science'. That is why today so many things which are left out of the official scientific view in the West are creeping up in the form of occult sciences, against whose rise modern science has no power at all. The totalitarian character of modern science has duped the vast majority of men who accept its point of view unconditionally into denying the possibility of any other form of knowledge of a serious order, with the result that interest in anything other than the 'official science' usually manifests itself in the form of a truncated and mutilated occultism. To quote the words of one of the rare men in the West who understand the real meaning of the Eastern traditions and their sciences, 'It is man who has let himself be deceived by discoveries and inventions of a falsely totalitarian science, that is to say a science that does not recognize its own proper limits and for that same reason misses whatever lies beyond these limits.'[5]

The terms 'science' and 'pseudo-science' will bear a little closer examination. A traditional science of metals and minerals such as alchemy, or of sacred geography or of geomancy, is called pseudo-science in modern parlance without anyone bothering to examine the principles that lie behind it. For instance, it is undeniable that by applying what today is called science in the form of different engineering or architectural projects, modern man often produces monstrosities of ugliness, while in applying the so-called 'pseudo-sciences' of sacred geography and geomancy the Chinese and Japanese or the Persians and Arabs have produced some of the most beautiful buildings, gardens and city landscapes imaginable. The same would apply to the applications of chemistry and alchemy, respectively.

Before the fruits of these two types of science—one of which is honoured by being called 'true science' and the other denigrated by being called 'pseudo-science'—man instinctively feels that there is an aspect of nature which so-called pseudo-science, as it has existed in traditional civilizations and not in its current deformations in the Occident, takes into consideration and which modern official science has allowed to be neglected. It is the qualitative and spiritual element of nature which is the source of the beauty reflected in the Persian or Japanese garden and in works of a similar nature based upon the Eastern sciences; and it is precisely this element that is lacking in the creations of modern science. Moreover, this qualitative element is certainly present in nature itself and with as great a certainty absent from the fruits of modern technology. One could thus conclude that the qualitative element, reflected in the beauty and harmony observable within nature, is an ontological aspect of nature which no science of nature can ignore except at its own peril. It is also because of the presence of this element of complexity pertaining to the chain or community of life on this earth that is the source of the strength and survival of this community, even from a biological point of view. In

[5] F. Schuon, 'No Activity without Truth', *Studies in Comparative Religion*, 1969, p. 196.

contrast, because of the lack of this qualitative and spiritual element, the very complexity of technology is of a quite different order, and as a result is becoming ever more a source of danger and weakness for technological society.

People who speak of the fusion of the sciences of East and West must know that such a thing has certainly not yet occurred in our times.[6] Nor could it occur so long as the attitude of modern science remains what it is. Such a fusion could, in fact, only occur if modern science would agree to put aside its monopolistic point of view so that a science could be developed which would embrace the qualitative and spiritual elements in nature as well as the quantitative aspect of things. Such a science would of necessity be based upon a metaphysical and cosmological doctrine which would perceive the relativity of the relative and realize that the whole material plane of reality is but a speck of dust before the supra-sensible and supra-formal worlds that encompass it. It would also of necessity be combined with an attitude of contemplation toward nature rather than be wedded to the desire for its domination and conquest. This desire, to be sure, is a direct result of the fact that, for all his science of the reality that surrounds him, modern man remains totally ignorant of certain basic aspects of this reality.

The import of Eastern science to the contemporary problems caused by the applications of Western science in many different fields can be illustrated through the problem of the unicity of and interrelation between things. This simple principle, which lies at the heart of all Sufi doctrine, will also cast some light upon the nature of Eastern science itself, whose contents we certainly cannot even begin to analyse here. Until now, modern science has succeeded largely by turning its back upon the interrelation between different parts of nature and by isolating each segment of nature in order to be able to analyse and dissect it separately. Ideally, according to Newtonian physics, in studying a falling body we can only calculate the gravitational forces acting upon it by knowing the mass and distance of every particle of matter in the material Universe. But since this is impossible, we consider only the earth as the centre of attraction and forget about all the other parts of the material Universe. As a result, we are able to arrive at a precise numerical figure by applying the laws of Newton to the simplified case in question. Something has been gained through this method no doubt; but also something very fundamental has been lost and neglected, namely the basic truth that

[6] See A. K. Coomaraswamy, 'Gradation, Evolution, and Reincarnation', in *The Bugbear of Literacy*, London, 1949, pp. 122–30.

the simple falling body is related to all the particles of the Universe through a force which Plato would call *eros* and Ibn Sînâ *'ishq*.[7]

Formerly the loss of this aspect of the relation between things was considered trivial when compared with the gains of being able to have mathematical precision. But now that the application of this partial science of nature has destroyed so much of nature itself and threatens us with much worse calamities, and since furthermore the ecologists have discovered that the whole natural environment is a remarkably complex but harmonious whole in which nothing functions except in connection with the other parts, it has become clear how catastrophic this type of omission actually is. Only now after causing so much damage do we realize that in order to survive we must put a stop to the indiscriminate destruction of our natural environment and the waste of the resources which provide for our needs; we must face the fact that our needs and the sources that can provide for them are interconnected with other parts of nature, animate and inanimate, in a way that the present sciences of nature have failed to grasp fully as a result of their own self-imposed limitation.

In the West a poet like John Donne could write four centuries ago in one of his devotional verses, 'No man is an *Iland*, intire of it selfe; every man is a peece of the *Continent*, a part of the *maine*; if a *Clod* bee washed away by the *Sea*, *Europe* is the lesse.' Although here Donne is referring to humanity, his vision certainly did not exclude the whole of creation of which man is a part. At a later date, Romantic poets like Wordsworth could describe the awareness of the spirit infused in all forms of nature whereby these forms are integrated, an awareness that leads man to a sense of the Infinite, as the following lines of his show:

> The sense sublime
> Of something far more deeply interfused,
> Whose dwelling is the light of setting suns,
> And the round ocean and the living air,
> And the blue sky, and in the mind of man;
> A motion and a spirit, that impels
> All thinking things, all objects of all thoughts,
> And rolls through all things.
>
> (*Lines Composed above Tintern Abbey*)

[7] On the attraction between material particles which is known as love or *'ishq* see Ibn Sînâ, *Risâlah fi'l-'ishq*, trans. by E. L. Fackenheim, *Medieval Studies*, vol. 7, 1945, pp. 208–28; and Nasr, *An Introduction to Islamic Cosmological Doctrines* pp. 261–2.

Such views were considered by official Western science as no more than poetic images, having nothing to do with 'science', and the same applied to the utterances of other romantic poets like Shelley and Novalis who wrote about the spiritual aspect of nature and the interrelation between its parts: only now do ecologists realize how 'scientific' such poetic utterances really were! But neither then nor now, because of the lack of the appropriate metaphysical knowledge on the part of modern scientists and the absence of a living sapiential tradition to give intellectual support to such poetry could a firm intellectual basis be established for the views expressed poetically by Donne, Wordsworth and others.[8] Consequently, no means can be discovered through these channels to transform Western science in a way that is fundamental enough to enable it to take into serious consideration this sense of the interrelation between things—which of necessity also means the various levels of existence.

It is to the Eastern sciences that we must turn in order to discover a world view in which the principle of the interrelatedness of things plays a central part. The traditional sciences of nature exist for the express purpose of making known, rather than veiling, the unicity of nature, which derives directly from the unity of the Divine Principle, as all the masters of Islamic gnosis have declared.[9] In the case of the Islamic sciences, the sense of Unity pervades all things and all forms of knowledge, unity (*al-tawḥîd*) being the central axis around which everything revolves in the Islamic world-view. In Hinduism also the various traditional sciences contained in the *darshânas*, although separate outwardly, are based on the interrelatedness of all things and represent stages in the development of knowledge. As for the Chinese and Japanese traditions, there also the 'ten-thousand things' are related and belong in fact to a whole, so that every science of nature reflects in one way or another both heaven and earth, and through them the unity that transcends this polarity. An ancient Chinese sage, Sêng-chao, once said: 'Heaven and earth and I are of the same root, the ten-thousand things and I are of one substance.' The intuition of the oneness of the roots of things, reflecting the metaphysical principle of the 'transcendent unity of Being', forms the very matrix of the Eastern sciences of nature.

[8] In contrast, such Sufi verses as the famous line of Sa'dî, 'I am in love with the whole Universe because it comes from Him'(عاشقم برهمه عالم که همه عالم از او ست), are supported by rigorous metaphysical principles which make such poems not only beautiful poetic utterances but explications of the Truth in the dress of poetic imagery.

[9] See S. H. Nasr, *An Introduction to Islamic Cosmological Doctrines*, pp. 4 ff.

As far as the traditional civilizations and their sciences are concerned, Islam occupies a special position in its role as intermediary between the Eastern traditions and the West. In the same way that geographically Islam covers the middle belt of the world, intellectually and spiritually it occupies a position half way between the mental climate of the Occident and the intellectual climate of the Indian and Far Eastern worlds. The reference made in the Quran to the Islamic people as the 'people of the middle' alludes, among other things, to this truth.

The Islamic sciences, which were cultivated avidly for seven hundred years, from the third/ninth to the tenth/sixteenth centuries and even afterwards, are deeply related on the one hand to Western science in its medieval and Renaissance phases and on the other hand to the sciences of India and China. In fact, Islamic science was related to these sciences historically both in its genesis and in its later development. Islam created a science which must be considered as science according to whatever definition we give to this term, a science without which science in the West could not have developed, although modern Western science eventually adopted a completely different point of view. At the same time Islamic science did not bring into being a secular science independent of a spiritual vision of the Universe. It carefully guarded the proportions between things, giving the spiritual and material their proper due and always preserving in mind the hierarchy of being and knowledge, whereby the integration of the sciences of nature into a wisdom transcending all discursive thought was maintained. Furthermore, many of the leading Muslim scientists were Sufis, gnostics (*'ârifs*), theosophers and traditional philosophers (*ḥakîms*) who developed the discursive and analytical sciences always in the bosom of the contemplative vision of nature.[10] From Ibn Sînâ to Naṣîr al-Dîn Ṭûsî and Quṭb al-Dîn Shîrâzî, all of whom were great scientists and philosopher-mystics, we encounter outstanding figures in the history of science who were at the same time men of spiritual vision and who would have felt perfectly at ease in the presence of the contemplative sages of China, Japan and India.

Islam developed within itself different intellectual schools, hierarchically ordered, which stretch over a vast intellectual expanse, ranging from Sufism, which is akin in its doctrines and methods to the pure sapiential doctrines of the Indian, Chinese and Japanese traditions, to the Peripatetic school, which is close to the main philosophical tradition of medieval Europe, from which sprang—albeit

[10] We have dealt extensively with this problem in our *Science and Civilization in Islam.*

through miscomprehension—modern rationalistic philosophy. Also, because of the centrality of the doctrine of unity in Islam, the principle of the unicity of nature upon which the Eastern sciences are based is emphasized with remarkable persistence in Islamic science, clothed in a rational as well as an intuitive garb. Thus it is perhaps more accessible to minds nurtured on Western modes of thought than the purely metaphysical and supra-rational perspectives usually found in the works of the sages of India and the Far East. But this is only a question of method of exposition and means of access to the pure truth. As already mentioned, the Eastern sciences are essentially unified in their vision of nature and in the principles of science based upon this vision.

To come back to the necessity of turning to Eastern science in order to help solve the crisis that Western science has brought upon itself, it must be stated that the realization by modern ecologists that one must study the whole environment as a complex unity in which everything is interrelated can only be complete if it also embraces the psychological and spiritual levels of reality and hence ultimately the Source of all that is. It is of course good to realize that inanimate objects are related to animate ones and that all parts of this corporeal world are interrelated; but the metaphysical principle of the relation of the states of being to one other, according to which any lower state of being derives its reality from the state above it, from which it is inseparable, has to be borne in mind at every step and can never be negated or nullified. If the terrestrial sphere has fallen into the danger of disorder and chaos, it is precisely because Western man has tried for several centuries to remain a purely terrestrial being and has sought to cut off his terrestial world from any reality that transcends it. The profanation of nature through its so-called conquest and the development of a purely secular science of nature would not have been possible otherwise.

This being so, it is not possible to correct this disorder in the natural domain without removing its cause, which is none other than the attempt to consider the terrestrial state of existence in isolation from all that transcends it. Present ecological considerations can overcome some of the barriers that separative and compartmentalized studies of nature have brought about, but they cannot solve the profounder problems which involve man himself, because it is precisely man who has disturbed the ecological balance through factors of a non-biological nature. The spiritual revolt of man against heaven has polluted the earth, and no attempt to rectify the situation on earth can ever be fully successful without the revolt against heaven coming to an end. For it is only the light of heaven cast upon the earth through the presence of seers and contemplatives living within the framework of the authentic religious traditions of humanity that preserves the harmony and beauty of nature and in fact maintains the cosmic equilibrium. Until this truth is understood all attempts to re-establish peace with nature will end in failure, although they can have partial success in preventing a particular tragedy from occurring here or there.

Once again it is only Eastern science, grounded in metaphysical principles, that can re-establish harmony between man and earth, by first establishing harmony between man and heaven and thereby turning man's covetous and greedy attitude toward nature, which underlies the reckless exploitation of natural resources into an attitude combined with and based upon contemplation and compassion. It is only tradition that can convert man from his role of plunderer of the earth to that of the 'vicegerent of God on earth' (*khalîfat Allâh fi'l-arḍ*), to use the Islamic terminology.[11]

If it be asked what one is to do in a practical manner in the present context, it can be answered that on the plane of knowledge one must seek a higher science of nature into which the quantitative sciences of nature can be integrated. This in turn can only be achieved through a knowledge of the indispensable metaphysical principles upon which these sciences are ultimately based. On the plane of action it would mean first of all to act at all times according to the truth, according to the religious principle, in whatever situation one is placed. The question often asked in desperation, as to whether activity still has any meaning, can best be answered once again in the words of F. Schuon, 'To this it must be answered that an affirmation of the truth, or any effort on behalf of truth, is never in vain, even if we cannot from beforehand measure the value or the outcome of such an activity. Moreover we have no choice in the matter. Once we know the truth we must needs live in it and fight for it, but what we must avoid at any price is to let ourselves bask in illusions. Even if, at this moment the horizon seems as dark as possible, one must not forget that in a perhaps unavoidably distant future the victory is ours and cannot but be ours. Truth by its very nature conquers all obstacles: *Vincit omnia Veritas*.[12]

As far as nature is concerned, for those who understand Sufism,

[11] See S. H. Nasr, 'Who is Man: the Perennial Answer of Islam', in *Man and His World*, Toronto, 1968, pp. 61–8, also in *Studies in Comparative Religion*, 1968, pp. 45–56.

[12] F. Schuon, 'No Activity without Truth,' p. 203.

or more generally metaphysics and the Eastern sciences of nature, it is their duty and function in relation to the truth to continue to expound their knowledge, to love nature and to contemplate her never-ending forms as theophanies of the Divine All-Possibility. Such an attitude would itself be the greatest charity for the world, for it would make concretely evident before modern man the possibility of another attitude towards nature, one which he needs desperately in order to survive even physically. Men from such cultures as the Islamic, where Sufi poets, especially those of the Persian language, have sung over the centuries of the beauties of nature as reflections of the beauties of paradise in which man's being is refreshed and renewed, have a special vocation at the present time. The same can be said of the Japanese whose remarkable artistic gifts combined with the deepest insight into nature have evolved what might be described as echoes of the angelic world amidst the very forms of earthly nature; Japanese artists have almost succeeded in bringing paradise literally down to earth. All who have been granted this insight must remain true to themselves and preserve the traditional sciences of nature and those metaphysical principles that are so precious for the future of their own cultures. They must also make these teachings well enough known to the world at large for others who are seeking such teachings to benefit from them. In this vital question, as in so many others, the traditional cultures of the East can render the greatest service to the world by remaining first of all faithful, more than ever before, to their own principles. And in this task they have the guarantee of ultimate success, for they are grounded in the truth, and as the Quran has said, 'Truth has come and falsehood has vanished away. Lo! falsehood is ever bound to vanish' (XVII, 81).

XI

What Does Islam Have to Offer to the Modern World?

One speaks so often today of this or that idea or element as being no longer pertinent to the modern world that one is apt to forget the essential reality of those doctrines and ideas which are of permanent significance; by overlooking the real needs of the modern world, one likewise overlooks the pertinence of the above ideas to those very needs. Whatever is not fashionable in this whirling pace of superficial change is considered unimportant and irrelevant; but what is, in fact, trivial and irrelevant is precisely that climate of thought which rejects and ignores the perennial and permanent truths that have always had meaning for men because they appeal to something permanent in man himself. If a whole section of modern humanity no longer finds the perennial truths of religion and the wisdom that has been cultivated and followed by sages throughout the ages meaningful, this loss of intellectual vision is most of all due to the fact that the very existence of this section of humanity has itself ceased to have much meaning. Taking itself and its imperfect perception of things, which it calls the 'existential predicament of modern man', too seriously, this type of man is not able to turn the sharp edge of its criticism toward itself and so does no more than criticize the objective and revealed truth contained in all the orthodox and authentic religions, which in reality are themselves the only possible judge and criterion of man's worth and value.

The pertinence of Islam to the modern world, as the pertinence of any other authentic religion, must be discussed in the light of the ontological priority of the one to the other; that is, Islam or, more generally, religion issues from the absolutely Real and is the message of Heaven, whereas the world as such is always relative and whether it be modern or ancient remains the 'world' (*dunyâ* in traditional Islamic language). The modern world is no less 'the world' than 'the world' to which traditional religious imagery refers. In fact it is farther removed from the Immutable and the Permanent than any other 'world' of which we have historical knowledge, and is therefore even more in need of the message of the Immutable.[1]

[1] See F. Schuon, *Light on the Ancient Worlds*, chapters I and II.

Islam is precisely such a message. It is the direct call of the Absolute to man inviting him to cease his wandering in the labyrinth of the relative and to return to the Absolute and the One; it appeals to what is most permanent and immutable in man.[2] And because it is such a message it is of pertinence to all 'worlds' and generations as long as man remains man. Today, even in academic circles in the West so long dominated by the evolutionism of the nineteenth century, certain scholars and scientists are beginning to rediscover and confirm the permanent nature of man and his needs, and to focus their attention on the permanent elements to which the Islamic message addresses itself most directly.[3] Men are born, live, and die and are always in quest of meaning, both for the *alpha* and the *omega* of their life and the period in between. This quest for meaning, which is as essential as the need for food and shelter, is in reality the quest for the Ultimate, for the Absolute, and it is as permanent a need of man as his need for nourishment. Religion provides precisely this meaning and in a sense is the shelter in the storm of the multiplicity and indefinity of cosmic manifestation and the uncertainties of temporal and terrestrial existence. It is not accidental that the Islamic prayers have been considered by certain Muslim sages as a refuge (*malja'*) in the storm of daily life. The message of Islam is as enduring as the need of man for this spiritual 'shelter' and for meaning in his human existence.

From a more specific point of view Islam remedies one of the particular maladies of the modern world, which is over-secularization, a process which is nothing else than depleting things of their spiritual significance. In the West it was first the temporal realm having to do with government and rule that came to be considered as secular,

[2] 'Islam is the meeting between God as such and man as such. God as such: that is to say God envisaged, not as He manifested Himself in a particular way but inasmuch as He is what He is and also inasmuch as by His nature He creates and reveals.

'Man as such: that is to say man envisaged, not as a fallen being needing a miracle to save him, but as man, a theomorphic being endowed with an intelligence capable of conceiving of the Absolute and with a will capable of choosing what leads to the Absolute.' F. Schuon, *Understanding Islam*, p. 13. See also S. H. Nasr, *Ideals and Realities of Islam*, chapter I.

[3] See, for example, J. Servier, *L'Homme et l'invisible*, which brings so much ethnological and anthropological evidence in favour of the essentially permanent nature of man throughout the ages. It is significant that only recently the Instituto Accademico di Roma under the direction of Professor Elémire Zolla organized for the first time in recent years a full symposium on the question of permanent values in historical process. See *I. valori permanente nel divenire storico*, Rome, 1969. A leading American scientist, Prof. David Hamburg of Stanford University, said only recently, 'The best relic we have of early man is modern man.'

although in the Middle Ages and in fact up to recent periods, as long as traditional political institutions survived, even the temporal possessed a religious significance.[4] Then 'thought' became secularized in the form of a secular philosophy and science, then art in all its branches followed suit and now finally religion itself has succumbed to the same tendency. The revolt of the Renaissance made this process appear at first as a gradual movement toward the attainment of freedom; but now that the process has reached such a dangerous impasse many realize that what the Renaissance made possible was only the freedom to lose the possibility of the attainment of the only real freedom open to man, namely the freedom of spiritual deliverance. Every other apparent freedom is no more than slavery either to outward natural forces or to inner passions.

Against this malady of over-secularization and this negative freedom which now verges upon anarchy, Islam presents a view of life which is completely sacred and a freedom which begins with submission to the Divine Will in order to open upwards towards the Infinite. In fact, in the languages of the Islamic peoples, there is no distinction between the sacred and the profane or temporal realm; appropriate terms do not even exist to translate such concepts.[5] Through the Divine Law or *Sharî'ah*, which encompasses all human life, every human activity is given a transcendent dimension; it is made sacred and thereby meaningful. Obviously this implies that one has accepted the *Sharî'ah* and is applying it, and therefore making a sacrifice from the point of view of human nature. But then one cannot make anything sacred without some form of sacrifice, for what does sacrifice mean but literally to make sacred, *sacrum-facere*? It always surprises a non-Muslim to observe to what extent Islamic society has been able to apply the *Sharî'ah* and how even in those regions where in modern times its hold has weakened among certain classes of Muslims, the attitudes which it has cultivated still endure.[6]

At the heart of the *Sharî'ah* lie the daily Muslim rites or *ṣalât* (*namâz* in Persian and Urdu), which according to prophetic tradition are the support and pillar of religion (*rukn al-dîn* or *'imâd al-dîn*). Now, one of the remarkable characteristics of this ritual activity, which corresponds not to the individual prayers of other religions such as

[4] See S. H. Nasr, 'Spiritual and Temporal Authority in Islam' in *Islamic Studies*, pp. 6–13.

[5] See S. H. Nasr, 'Religion and Secularism, their Meaning and Manifestation in Islamic History', in *Islamic Studies*, pp. 14–25.

[6] Concerning the significance of the *Sharî'ah* in Islam see S. H. Nasr, *Ideals and Realities of Islam*, chapter IV.

Christianity, but to a rite such as the mass, is that it can be performed anywhere and by any Muslim. The sacerdotal function, which in certain religions is relegated to a particular class of men, is shared in Islam among all members of the community, giving the possibility to members of the Islamic faith to remain a part of the community of believers, the *ummah,* without needing to be geographically attached to it. Thus, in an age such as the present, when men travel far and often and where circumstances may render certain religious practices difficult, Islam possesses the relative advantage of being practicable anywhere.

The fact that Islam possesses this power of adaptation to an eminent degree does not of course mean that a Muslim should conform to the modern world and all the errors that it comprises. Islam, like every other revealed truth, comes from God. Therefore, it is the world that must be made to conform to this truth and not vice versa. With this provision in mind it can be said, however, that in whatever situation he is placed, the man desirous of practising Islam can do so without encountering the outward difficulties which beset certain religions, especially those where continuous daily rituals form an important part of religious life.

The daily Muslim rites also bestow the great advantage upon man of being able to carry his centre with him. The great malady of modern man can be reduced to his loss of centre, a loss which is so clearly depicted in the chaotic so-called literature and art of modern times. Islam offers the direct remedy to this illness. In general, prayer places man in the axial and vertical dimension which points to the Centre. In particular, the Islamic rites make possible the 'carrying' of this Centre wherever one goes. The fact that wherever one may be on earth, the daily prayers are directed toward Mecca, the supreme centre of Islam, indicates clearly this reflection of the Centre whenever and wherever one happens to be praying. By virtue of the power of these prayers man continues to be attached to the Centre which coordinates and harmonizes his activity and his life.

The cardinal Islamic doctrine of unity (*al-tawḥîd*) itself emphasizes the necessity for integration. God is One and so man, who is created in 'His Form', must become integrated and unified. The goal of the religious and spiritual life, as already pointed out, must be the complete and total integration of man in all his depth and amplitude.[7] Modern man suffers from excessive compartmentalizing in his science and education as well as in his social life. Through the very pressure of technology, social bonds and even the human personality tend to

[7] See the chapter 'Sufism and the Integration of Man' in this book.

disintegrate. The Islamic ideal of unity stands in stark opposition to this multiplicity and division, reversing the centrifugal tendencies of man which make him ever more prone to dissipate his soul and energy toward the periphery, and returning the soul to the Centre.

Today everyone cries for peace but peace is never achieved, precisely because it is metaphysically absurd to expect a civilization that has forgotten God to possess peace. Peace in the human order results from peace with God and also with nature.[8] It is the result of the equilibrium and harmony which can come into being only through the integration made possible by *tawḥîd*. Islam has quite unjustly been depicted as a religion of the sword and of war whereas it is a religion which seeks to bring about peace through submission to the Will of God, as the name *islâm*, in Arabic meaning both peace and submission, indicates; and this is only made possible by giving each thing its due. Islam preserves a remarkable equilibrium between the needs of the body and those of the spirit, between this world and the next. No peace is possible in a civilization which has reduced all human welfare to animal needs and refuses to consider the needs of man beyond his earthly existence. Moreover, having reduced man to a purely terrestrial being, such a civilization is not able to provide for the spiritual needs which nevertheless continue to exist, with the result that there is created a combination of crass materialism and an even more dangerous pseudo-spiritualism, whose opposition to materialism is more imaginary than real.[9] And thus we are faced with the endangering of even the terrestrial life which today has come to be cherished as the final end in itself. One of the basic messages of Islam to the modern world is its emphasis on the importance of giving each thing its due, of preserving each element in its place, of guarding the just proportion between things. The peace that men seek is only possible if the total needs of man, not only in his capacity of a thinking animal but also as a being born for immortality, are considered. To be concerned only with the physical needs of men is to reduce men to slavery and to produce problems even on the physical plane that are impossible of solution. It is not religion but modern medicine that has created the problem of over-population. But now religion is asked to solve this problem by accepting to forgo the sacred meaning of human life itself, if not totally, at least in part.

Likewise of vital concern today is peace between religions. In this

[8] See S. H. Nasr, *The Encounter of Man and Nature*, chapter IV.

[9] Concerning the stages of revolt against true spirituality leading through materialism to pseudo-spiritualism see R. Guénon, *The Reign of Quantity and the Signs of the Times*, pp. 229 ff.

domain also Islam has a particular message for modern man. As pointed out in a previous chapter, Islam considers the acceptance of anterior prophets as a necessary article of faith (*îmân*) in Islam itself and asserts quite vigorously the universality of revelation.[10] No other sacred text speaks as much and as openly of the universality of religion as the Quran. Islam, the last of the religions of the present humanity, here joins with Hinduism, the first and most primordial of existing religions, in envisaging religion in its universal manifestation throughout the cycles of human history. As the discussion in chapter IX has shown, in the metaphysics and theology of comparative religion Islam has a great deal to teach those who wish to study the subject on a more serious plane than just collecting historical and philological facts.

Finally, in discussing this theme of peace, something must be said of the inner peace which men seek desperately today, desperately enough to have caused a whole army of pseudo-yogis and spiritual healers to establish themselves in the West. Men now feel instinctively the importance of meditation and contemplation but alas only too few are willing to undergo the discipline in the fold of an authentic tradition which can alone guarantee them access to the joy made possible through the contemplation of the celestial realities. Thus they turn to drugs or self-realization centres or the thousand and one 'pseudo-masters' from the East—a veritable revenge upon the West for all that was done to Oriental traditions during the colonial period.[11]

Islam possesses all the means necessary for spiritual realization in the highest sense; Sufism is the chosen vehicle of these means. Now because Sufism is the esoteric and inner dimension of Islam it cannot be practised apart from Islam; only Islam can lead those who have the necessary aptitude to this inner court of joy and peace that is Sufism and which is the foretaste of the 'gardens of paradise'. Here again the characteristic of the contemplative way of Islam, or Sufism, is that it can be practised anywhere and in every walk of life. Sufism is not based on outer withdrawal from the world but on inner detachment.

[10] See the chapter 'Islam and the Encounter of Religions' in this book. For a more general discussion of this question see F. Schuon, *The Transcendent Unity of Religions*.

[11] Unfortunately certain pseudo-Sufis are beginning to do much harm to the cause of Sufism in Europe today. Their first error is to seek to detach Sufism from Islam, thereby turning it into an occultism devoid of any spiritual interest and in most cases psychically dangerous. The falsity of their extravagant claims is seen most clearly in the pitiful results achieved in the name of these travesties of Sufism. The tree is always judged by the fruit it bears.

As a contemporary Sufi has said, 'It is not I who have left the world, it is the world that has left me.' The inner detachment may in fact be combined with intense outward activity. Sufism achieves the wedding of the active and contemplative lives consonantly with the unifying nature of Islam itself. The spiritual force of Islam creates through intense activity a climate in the outer world, a climate which naturally attracts man towards meditation and contemplation, as is seen so clearly in the spirit of Islamic art.[12] The outward opposition with which by definition the world of activity is concerned is resolved in an inner peace which is a characteristic of the One, of the Centre.

Islam, like all other authentic religions, bears a message from the eternal directed to that which is immutable and permanent in man. As such it knows no temporality. But in addition it possesses certain characteristics, placed there providentially, to enable men in any circumstances and in any 'world' to be able to follow it and to benefit from its teachings. Were there ever to be a world for which religion in general and Islam in particular had no meaning at all, that world would itself cease to possess any meaning: it would become sheer illusion. As long as there is any element of reality attaching to *the* world, or to such and such *a* world, Islam will continue to possess a valid message for that world, a message which is real just because it comes from the Truth for, as the Islamic metaphysical doctrines teach us, Truth and Reality are ultimately one.

[12] On the spiritual principles of Islamic art see T. Burckhardt, 'Perennial Values of Islamic Art', *Studies in Comparative Religion*, Summer, 1967, pp. 132–41. See also T. Burckhardt, *Sacred Art in East and West*, London, 1967, chapter IV.

INDEX

Ābādihī, Mullā Muḥammad Ja'far, 102
Abbasid period, 135
'Abd al-Jabbār, Qāḍī, 135
'Abd al-Karīm al-Jīlī, v. al-Jīlī,
'Abd al-Laṭīf, Shāh, 20
'Abd al-Razzāq al-Kāshānī, v. al-Kāshānī,
Abi dharma, 142
Abraham, 130, 139, 140
Abrahamic, 130, 131, 134
Abrahamic tradition, 138, 144
Abū Dharr, 114
Abu'l-Faḍl, 139
Abu'l-Ḥasan al-Ash'arī, v. al-Ash'arī
Abū Naṣr al-Sarrāj, 76
Abū Sa'īd ibn Abi'l-Khayr, 77, 78, 82
Abū Yazīd Basṭāmī, v. Bāyazīd Baṣṭāmī,
Adam, 63, 82, 131, 132
al-Adham, Ibrāhīm, 114
Ādhar Kaywān, 138
al-adwār, 91
Afandī, v. Bālī Afandī,
Afghan, 119
Afghanistan, 133
al-Aflākī, 14
afrād, 119
ahl al-bayt, 116
ahl al-ḥaqq, 73
ahl al-kitāb, 132, 139
Ahmad, A., 139
aḥsan taqwīm, 25, 26, 32-34
aḥwāl, 18, 72, 73, 76, 77, 82, 119
al-ākhirah, 54
al-akwār, 91
'Alā' al-Dawlah Simnānī, v. Simnānī,
'Ālam ārā-yi 'abbāsī, 117
al-'Alawī, Shaykh Aḥmad, 35, 136
Alchemie, Sinn und Weltbild, 88
alchemy, 18, 40, 48, 156
Aleppo, 116
Algerian, 136
'Alī (ibn Abī Ṭālib), 19, 66, 106–110, 113–115, 117
'Alī al-Riḍā (Imām Riḍā), 114
'Alids, 117
'ālim, 115
Allah, 50, 53, 78, 93
amānah, 26
America, 145
American Indians, 145
'Āmilī, Bahā' al-Dīn, 118
Amīr Khusraw (Dihlawī), 20, 139
'Ammār al-Yāsir, 114
Āmulī, Sayyid Ḥaydar, 100, 108, 110, 111, 115, 116
Anatolian Turks, 117
anbiyā', 148
Andrae, T., 105
angelology, 138
anima, 68
Anquetil-Dupérron, 140
Anṣārī, Khwājah 'Abdallāh, 34, 77
anthropology, 90, 131
Antiquity, 53
Apostolic succession, 104
Āqāsī, Ḥājj Mīrzā, 119
'aql, 54, 55
'aql-i juz'ī, 55
al-'aql al-kullī (*'aql-i kullī*), 54, 55
al-'aql al-salīm, 55
Arab, 13, 102, 113, 137
Arab Near East, 13, 137
Arabia, 139
Arabic, 14, 18–20, 33, 57, 71, 74, 102, 113, 131, 139, 142, 145, 168
Arabs, 14, 156
'Arāqī, Fakhr al-Dīn, 98
arba'īnāt, 65
Arberry, A. J., 15, 34, 59, 72, 76, 78, 150
architecture, 19, 20
'ārif, 115, 160
Aristotle, 53, 92
Aristotelian rationalism, 53
al-'arsh, 88
'arsh al-raḥmān, 36
Art and Thought, 140
asfal sāfilīn, 25, 26, 32, 33
Asfār, 100
aṣḥāb al-budadah, 142
aṣḥāb al-ṣuffah, 114